Series 7 **Exam Prep**
2024-2025

Study Guide with 375 Practice Questions and Answer Explanations for the FINRA General Securities Representative Certification

HANLEY
TEST PREPARATION

Contents

Free Video Offer!

Thank you for purchasing from Hanley Test Preparation! We're honored to help you prepare for your exam. To show our appreciation, we're offering an Exclusive Test Tips Video.

This video includes multiple strategies that will make you successful on your big exam.

All we ask is that you email us your feedback and describe your experience with our product. Amazing, awful, or just so-so. We want to hear what you have to say!

To get your FREE VIDEO, just send us an email at bonusvideo@hanleytestprep.com with **Free Video** in the subject line and the following information in the body of the email:

- The name of the product you purchased
- Your product rating on a scale of 1-5, with 5 being the highest rating.
- Your feedback about the product.

If you have any questions or concerns, please don't hesitate to contact us at
support@hanleytestprep.com

Thanks again!

Introduction

Who doesn't want to understand and, better still, work in the charged atmosphere of the US stock market? It's the most happening industry in the world where you deal with real people's dreams and ambitions. Access to this high-quality world cannot be easy, and no matter your banking experiences, you must go through the tough Series 7 and qualify. The question is *how to*?

The Series 7 license exam is the General Securities Representative Examination (GS) on a candidate's knowledge to sell securities, municipal bonds, investment company securities, variable annuities, direct participation programs, options, and government securities. The Financial Industry Regulatory Authority (FINRA) administers the Series 7 examination. Passing Series 7 is necessary for aspirants to legally trade US securities, advise the sale of securities, or work as validated analysts.

The Series 7 license remains valid if you work for a FINRA-member firm or self-regulatory organization (SRO). The license expires if a member is terminated or leaves a firm and cannot get reemployed within two years at another FINRA-member firm or SRO.

Isn't a Series 6 license sufficient? Although both allow you to serve as a financial guide to your clients, Series 6 is much more restricted. It entitles you as a limited representative when you can only sell mutual funds, variable annuities, and insurance premiums. A Series 7 license, conversely, offers you a broader work area. Your designation as a *stockbroker* by FINRA instantly buys recognition from investment firms and banks.

If you have a different securities license, you still need to take the Series 7 if you want to be involved in selling a wide range of securities except commodities futures, real estate, and life insurance. However, note that the Securities Industry Essentials (SIE) and Series 7 top-off exams are "co-requisites."

So, how do you start? Before the test, a FINRA member firm or SRO must sponsor you. After a four-month stint or more, you can file Form U4 (Uniform Application for Securities Industry Registration), which will register you for the exam. Most hiring/training firms have a mandatory Series 7 licensing program in their training package.

Anyone over 18 is eligible to take the examination. Although there are no education requirements for the Series 7 exam, most candidates have a college degree in a finance-related field. You can take and pass SIE and Series 7 in any order, but you must take both. Since the SIE exam doesn't need sponsorship, it's logical to take it first. The steps are as follows:

1. Taking and passing the SIE exam.
2. Securing a sponsorship from a FINRA-member firm.
3. Registering for the Series 7 exam.
4. Studying for and passing the Series 7 exam.

How tough is the exam?

- You must be able to apply your knowledge and concepts of securities to specific scenarios that the test taker will examine. The detailed questions are on the day-to-day activities, responsibilities, and job roles of representatives and are challenging.
- Within 3 hours and 45 minutes, you must correctly answer at least 90 questions (72%) out of 125 scorable questions. The test proceeds in a bell curve, starting and finishing with easier ones, with the most challenging ones in between.
- Failing the test means you must wait 30 days before retaking it. Each time, you'll pay the test fee of $300. Successively failing on three occasions increases the wait period to 180 days.

Do not take the Series 7 exam lightly. It requires learning techniques, knowledge, and skills to navigate complex questions in an examination setting. As it is, stress levels escalate during examinations. Solving financial calculations such as options pricing, bond yields, margin calculations, and regulatory computations, among other topics, is challenging. These calculations need intricate formulas and a deep understanding of mathematical principles.

Not everyone is comfortable with mathematical concepts; the timed test makes it all the more challenging. It adds another layer to an efficient test-taking strategy: time management. You must learn these crucial skills systematically during the preparation process.

Test preparation is hardly limited to acquiring knowledge. It also encompasses taking mock tests, managing time, and managing stress and expectations.

At no point can you allow self-doubt. It's difficult but not impossible. And life becomes more interesting when you face a challenge.

But facing a challenge without a proper blueprint is unwise. To crack the Series 7, a thorough and well-thought-out guidebook should be your blueprint.

Throughout your journey, this guidebook will offer you practical tips and insights to thrive and flourish. Its aim is to keep your intellectual and psychological dispositions high. If you want to achieve your ambition, our efforts equip you with the knowledge and strategies to succeed. It includes:

- A complete set of Series 7 FAQs and Tips
- A comprehensive set of study materials covering all the crucial topics of the four major functions of a General Securities Representative
- Three full-length tests based on realistic scenarios per actual Series 7 test
- A distinctive and comprehensive study approach

Collectively, these features make it a robust and valuable resource necessary to complete the Series 7 exam successfully.

As your confidence grows with this study material, you will realize that you just need a catalyst: this book. If achieving results had been difficult before this book, make it possible with the new information I have accumulated in this book.

Let's begin our journey together, which we are convinced will conclude with your achievement.

Chapter One: Important Tips on How to Crack Series 7 in One Attempt

This chapter is on the frequently asked questions (FAQs) about the Series 7. It will equip you with strategic tips to optimize your test preparation. The information shared is basic. Nevertheless, it helps you form a solid foundation for passing the examination successfully.

The Series 7 Exam and License

The Series 7 exam evaluates the competency of entry-level General Securities Representatives for which you must pass both the Series 7 exam and a general knowledge co-requisite, the Securities Industry Essentials (SIE) exam. Of all the different series, the Series 7, being versatile and widely applicable, is the most common FINRA Top-Off exam passed. It confers the designation of a registered representative, commonly referred to as a financial advisor and stockbroker.

The exam consists of 125 multiple-choice questions. Each question has four answer choices. There are 10 additional unidentified and unscored pretest questions randomly distributed throughout the test. It means the exam comprises a total of 135 items (125 scored and 10 unscored) in 3 hours and 45 minutes.

The Series 7 exam includes topics like investment risk, taxation, equity and debt instruments, packaged securities, options, retirement plans, and client interactions. The test ensures that you understand the nature of these securities and financial instruments and knowledge concerning general securities representatives' day-to-day activities, responsibilities, and job functions. The following table highlights the test topics, their weight, and the number of questions asked. Each section has specific knowledge domains and regulation sets (Series 7 Content Outline.pdf, 2021).

Sections	Exam percentage	Number of questions asked
1 - Seeks Business for the Broker-Dealer from Customers and Potential Customers	7%	9
2 - Opens Accounts after Obtaining and Evaluating Customers' Financial Profile and Investment Objectives	9%	11
3 - Provides Customers with Information About Investments, Makes Suitable Recommendations, Transfers Assets and Maintains Appropriate Records	73%	91
4 - Obtains and Verifies Customers' Purchase and Sales Instructions and Agreements; Processes, Completes and Confirms Transactions	11%	14
Total	100%	125

A Prometric testing center administers the test by computer, and the third-party proctor conducts the online examination. You will have a tutorial on taking the exam before the test begins.

The Best Test Practices

Preparing for a competitive test requires thorough planning, like drafting a battle strategy. You must analyze strengths and weaknesses, identify priority areas, and know how to pinpoint and develop tactics to handle challenging questions. Essential skills also include:

- Choosing appropriate study materials.
- Preparing a robust question data bank.
- Taking plenty of mock tests.
- Managing time efficiently.
- Creating flexible study time.

You should attempt all the questions; there is no penalty for guessing. A statistical adjustment process known as equating standardizes test scores of all candidates by placing the scores on a common scale. It accounts for the slight differences in complexity that may exist among the different sets of exam items the candidates receive. Regardless of the exam set, you are assured a fair comparison of scores weighted by the same passing standard (Series 7 Content Outline, 2021).

You cannot bring reference materials to the testing session. Penalties for cheating or attempting to cheat on the test are severe. The pass rate for Series 7 is 65%, with a first-time pass rate of 60%–70%. Those who fail may find the exam too difficult or have had less than adequate preparation time. Both are resolvable. While you can take the test again, it may seem very difficult if you're unprepared. It underscores the necessity to adopt the best test practices.

Study Tools

Read the comprehensive guidebooks thoroughly, referring to standard textbooks whenever necessary. Make notes in the margins or a separate notebook, manual or digital. Utilize the graphics and exercises that help you learn and retain faster and better. This guidebook gives special emphasis on information that is likely to appear on the test. Practice reading with flashcards, tests, and real-life examples.

An overview of the exam outline helps in planning. Analyze the weight each section receives to plan your strategy. Determine how you will handle each study group, digest new material, and allocate time to each assignment to meet minor goals.

Planning and organization reduce exam stress. Knowledge-based exams seldom benefit from last-minute preparations. Read each section thoroughly, and set the objective for the day. You must stick to them, which requires discipline. Study in peace, quiet, and without interruptions to maximize your efforts. Let's highlight the key features of a good study habits:

1. Group learning *with common goals* helps share ideas and reduce stress. Discuss your readings with classmates or educate younger colleagues. These discussions improve memory and field knowledge.
2. Imagine how things connect. Conceptualization, from a larger viewpoint, *promotes intuitive learning*. Make flowcharts to practice solving multi-component issues. Combining knowledge from several sources and their constant updates is useful.
3. Get comfortable with each unit until you're ready to move on. Mastering every subject is not an ideal situation. Seek additional and relevant information to link materials with a common thread. It will help you remember and associate information.
4. Write down formulas and key points on Post-it notes. Stick them where you can see them. Visualizing them helps you memorize.

Prioritizing Study

Landing with an ocean of materials or wading through innumerable rules and regulations and keeping abreast of them, besides learning different formulas and mathematical calculations, requires the skill of a juggler. What you evidently need is prioritization of study. Which portions should you emphasize while brushing through some others? Concepts and work experiences in banking businesses, policies, and political scenarios help. Still, these are some tips that you may find useful:

1. Look for the information you do not know. You may use a daily retrieval practice. Question yourself on what you studied the previous day.

Document what you can answer correctly. However, your focus must be on incorrect answers. Instead of focusing on complex issues (which you will probably remember), focus on simple features like terms and concepts that you may miss during learning. In this way, construct a formative assessment opportunity on a piece of paper throughout a unit of study.

2. Next, consider the information you have answered correctly by guessing. It is an assumption of learning that you must address immediately and note. Mark the questions you guessed with an asterisk. A more substantial way to understand how much you know and how much you have guessed is to assign a confidence rating to all the questions you attempted. This scale can be random based on a scale of 1 to 10. A score of 1 can indicate no confidence and pure guess, while a score of 10 indicates full confidence. This method helps you to understand where you are regarding content knowledge.

3. One of the crucial aspects of prioritization is to clear areas of confusion or "mixed-up concepts." There can be a mix-up of two or more terms or ideas. In such instances, pause to think through. Also, talk aloud, emphasizing why you mixed them up to help them sort it out.

Time Management

1. Start studying well in advance to organize a schedule and maintain it. Effective time management could prevent spending hours studying.

2. Study subject matters in blocks. Limit the size of these blocks. Revise the previous day's information before studying new ones. This type of daily short and defined studying can help retention and reduce stress over remaining tasks.

3. How much do you need to study? About 100–120 hours of dedicated study time for 4–5 weeks should be sufficient. Take short, ten-minute breaks. Finish a chunk of material and allow your brain to process information.

4. Learning is best when one is rested and alert. Effective study time depends on individual choice, behavior, and other constraints. In general, study whenever you're most likely to understand and remember. Your brain being most receptive will lead to enhanced recall of facts.

Learning Style

1. Modality is selecting a method that suits specific learning styles. Learners can be visual, auditory, or tactile. Visual learners best study using color-coding, drawing, or applying symbols in their notes to remember an idea. Auditory learners learn better with a similar study companion or can read aloud.
2. Any learning style can use flashcards. Use free time to organize information for easy viewing. Use distinct colors for distinct categories.
3. Mnemonic devices may aid memory recall, such as a brief list with the same letter for each item.

Practice Tests

1. Take as many practice tests as possible.
2. Instead of taking multiple partial tests after finishing a section, take the whole test (135 questions) in 3 hours and 45 minutes.
3. The first test should be untimed, with the book open. Once you get habituated, time it.
4. Study text material before taking practice tests. At best, sample tests simulate exam patterns. They carefully prepare you to pass the actual test and be on schedule. However, not studying the material and memorizing sample questions and answers may be incorrect.
5. Practice exams allow you to evaluate your knowledge and find areas for improvement. Work on weaknesses like grasping the subject and terminology and improving speed and efficiency. Then, pinpoint problem areas by building customized exams based on the length and topic of your choice.
6. Questions may try to lead you to a choice. You should avoid the trap. Understand the context of the question before choosing an option. Such questions assess your domain knowledge.
7. Practice exams include a section explaining answer options. The explanations in the answer section should stimulate you to explore your study material and textbooks for further exploration. Explanations alone cannot help you grasp a concept that only touches on a portion of the question's context. Even if the explanation is clear, thoroughly explore all connected

ideas to ensure a complete grasp. This method of study will reinforce your memory.

8. Review weak units in the study materials. Study in like-minded groups, quiz your friends on different topics, and teach those interested in taking Series 7. All these attempts will help you to fortify your preparation.

Strategies For Test Day

1. Ensure you are well-rested on the test day.
2. Eat complex carbohydrates like wholegrain cereals for your breakfast.
3. Stay hydrated.
4. Carry your ID and valid documents.
5. Leave cell phones and study materials outside the exam area.

Test-Taking Strategy

1. Read the entire question carefully, even when you know the answer immediately.
2. Look for hedge clauses in the question that have things like "if, not, all, none, and except."
3. Set your pace depending on the time and the number of questions. The computer shows the remaining time. The pacing technique should start during preparation through mock tests. It cannot be mastered on the test day.
4. Answer the straightforward questions first.
5. Reserve some time for revision and answering complicated questions. Your aim during an examination is not to test your knowledge but to pass the test.
6. Questions may use unfamiliar language. Study the question's context or topic. Look for keywords like prospectus in the question, which can alert you about a new issue.
7. Answers with definitive words like precisely, invariably, etc., leave limited options.
8. Hedge words like may, can, sometimes, frequently, nearly, primarily, usually, generally, and seldom leave scope for possibilities.
9. Switchback words are but, although, nonetheless, on the other hand, even

though, in spite of, notwithstanding, and regardless. They change the question's meaning.

10. "Which of the following is not wrong?" "False" and "except for" bear confusing negative meanings.
11. Information in one question can help you answer a different question.
12. If you are unsure of an answer, your first guess is most likely correct. Modify your response only if you did not read the question correctly or if you find new or additional helpful information in another question. For guessing:

   a. Identify and eliminate incorrect answers.
   b. Start by eliminating the worst solution.
   c. Think carefully about the remaining options.
   d. Remove the second worst answer.
   e. Continue eliminating until you reach the most likely correct answer.

13. Benchmarking answers for multiple-choice questions involves choosing a plausible response as the benchmark and comparing it to others until you get the most logical answer, your new benchmark.
14. Avoid factual pitfalls. They are valid but inappropriate for the questions. Read the questions before and again after replying to see whether the answers match.
15. Many questions, mostly the stories, contain lengthy information, which is often the case in story problems. Separate the story from the question and identify what the question is asking.
16. Any requisite math is straightforward. Calculators are permitted; use them to avoid silly mistakes.

Series 7 is not just an exam to guarantee a stockbroker's position in the banking sector. FINRA member firms, investment banks, and financial institutions want to abide by the regulations and be on good terms with FINRA. Taking Series 7 is mandatory for finance professionals in portfolios other than buying or selling stocks, such as equity research, asset management, investment banking advisory services, etc.

That is why the exam focuses more on the various security types and financial instruments such as municipal securities, equities, bonds, or options. The emphasis is more on managing the practical aspects of these jobs in economic sectors. Passing the Series 7 entitles you to deal with the following products and activities:

1. Private placements of corporate securities and offerings for the public (stocks and bonds)
2. Warrants
3. Mutual funds
4. Money market funds
5. Unit investment trusts (UITs)
6. Exchange-traded funds (ETFs)
7. Real estate investment trusts (REITs)
8. Options on mortgage-backed securities
9. Securities of Government portfolios
10. Government securities Repos and certificates of accrual
11. Direct participation programs
12. Venture capital
13. Sale of municipal securities
14. Hedge funds

Chapter Two: Regulatory Framework and Conduct Rules

Each and every section of Series 7 contains associated conduct rules and broader securities regulations. These ensure compliance with the laws and observe ethical conduct. Gathering all of them in one place under a chapter will enable you to locate them quickly.

FINRA Conduct Rules

The FINRA website presents certain rules of conduct. Essentially, rules must bind any securities industry and regulations to ensure public safety and retain their faith in the industry. FINRA rules provide investor protection and uphold high standards of conduct and ethics of those working in the securities industry in the US. The scope for conduct obligations is binding in areas of honest dealing, accuracy of investment recommendations, and surveillance.

Proposed rules go through an internal reviewing process. They then go before the FINRA committees and to the FINRA board for possible publication of a regulatory notice. *Regulatory Notice* requests statements on a proposal within one to two months. FINRA has posted all comment letters on its website since December 1, 2003.

FINRA and other SRO rule filings occur electronically with the SEC instead of in paper form, effective November 2004. The SEC posts the rule for comment in the Federal Register and keeps it open for 21 days. It requests FINRA to respond to select comments based on their nature. Following final approval, the SEC officially announces the rule in the Federal Register. After SEC approval, FINRA publishes a *Regulatory Notice* informing SEC approval of the rule change and the effective date (FINRA Rule Making Process, n.d.).

Public Communication

Rule 2210 discusses:

1. Retail communications' approval, review, and recordkeeping.

   a. Institutional communications

2. Correspondence
3. Recordkeeping under SEA rule 17a-4(b)
4. Filing requirements and assessment processes

   a. Some members must file retail communications before first use
   b. Pre-use filing for some retail communications
   c. Television or video retail communications filing
   d. First use date and approval info
   e. On-spot inspection
   f. Filing exemptions
   g. Communications considered filed with FINRA

5. Content standards

FINRA Rule 2210 (Communications with the Public) divides communications into correspondence, retail, and institutional communications and sets principles-based content requirements to adapt to communications technology and practices. New members must submit retail communications with FINRA's Advertising Regulation Department in their first year.

FINRA Rule 2220 (Options Communications) controls members' public option communications. MSRB Rule G-21 (Advertising by Brokers, Dealers, or Municipal Securities Dealers) has comparable content criteria for municipal securities and municipal dealer services, amenities, and capacities (Communications with the Public, 2019).

Terms

1. Communication refers to correspondence, retail, and institutional communications.
2. Correspondence is circulating/providing any written (including electronic) transmission to 25 or fewer retail investors within 30 calendar days. Retail communication involves more than 25 retail investors.
3. Institutional written communication is distributed to institutional investors only (others are retail investors), not including members' internal communications.
4. Institutional investors:

    a. Individuals defined in Rule 4512(c), irrespective of an account with a member
    b. Governmental entity/ its subdivision
    c. Employee benefit plan(s) to employees under the same employer, fulfilling Section 403(b) or Section 457 of the Internal Revenue Code with at least 100 participants in the aggregate, but not any participant
    d. Qualified plan(s) under Exchange Act Section 3(a)(12)(C) with the same requirements
    e. Member or the member's registered person
    f. An individual operating on their own

No member may regard a message as sent to an institutional investor if they anticipate retail Investors will acquire it/be forwarded.

Exam findings

1. Insufficient communications fostering digital assets.
2. Deficient surveillance and recordkeeping for digital communications

    a. Not having policies and procedures to detect and react to red flags—such as client grievances, representatives' emails, OBA reviews, or advertising reviews.

b. Registered representatives used impermissible business-related digital communications methods like texting, messaging, social media, collaboration apps, or "electronic sales seminars" in chat rooms.

3. No written supervisory procedures (WSPs) and communications control that use non-member names (so-called "doing business as" or "dba" names) needed.

4. Distortions in cash management account communications

a. New product groups or divisions must evaluate Cash Management Accounts to ensure they can support business processes, supervisory infrastructure, accountability programs, and communications initiatives

5. Discourage the use of inaccurate, deceptive, and imprecise information in mobile apps.

Good Practices

FINRA found the following best procedures in its member firm examinations:

1. Maintaining and managing digital communication supervisory processes.
2. Designing supervisory review protocols for each digital channel, tool, and feature.
3. Creating WSPs and controls for live-streamed events, programmed presentations, and video blogs.
4. Establishing obligatory training programs before granting access to firm-approved digital channels, including business expectations and personal digital communications and how to use all channel capabilities.
5. Temporarily suspend or permanently bar registered representatives who violated the rules from particular digital channels or features, compelling them to attend further digital communications training.
6. Emphasizing the risks of digital assets to weigh against any statements or claims in a digital asset communication, such as that such investments are speculative, high-risk, illiquid, may have no value, lack regulatory certainty, may be subject to market tampering and can subject investors to principal loss.

7. Communication assessment by checking organizations' communications to ensure they weren't inflating digital asset advantages/project/platform status.
8. Having protocols for updating and executing procedures for outside business activity (OBA) names.

    a. Firm-approved suppliers must provide content or standardized forms with authorized information and disclosures for all OBA communications involving the broker-dealer's securities activity, including websites, social media, electronic documents, and others.
    b. Prohibit OBA communications affecting broker-dealer securities activity without compliance authorization and establish centralized review and approval mechanisms.

Registered representatives must inform compliance of allowed communication changes and review them yearly for updates.

Differentiating Digital Assets from Broker-Dealer Products via Communication:

1. The condition emphasizes recognition, discrimination, and distinction of broker-dealer products and services from those of affiliates or third parties, such as digital asset affiliates, including explicitly and strongly recognizing entities that manage non-securities digital assets businesses (and clarifying that such services were not offered by the broker-dealer or protected by securities regulations).

Using New Interactive, Game-Like Digital Platforms

Online brokers and options trading brought more ordinary investors into the markets in 2020. Many online broker-dealers, financial services, and consumer-based firms provide applications with interactive and "game-like" features and related advertising and marketing. They are how organizations publicize, develop accounts, offer clients investments, and state investment options.

Firms must regard the following features to meet regulatory compliance:

1. Comply with Reg BI and Form CRS requirements for any "recommenda-tion" requiring a broker-dealer to act in a retail customer's "best interest."
2. Disclose risks to consumers, fees, expenses, conflicts of interest, and re-quired norms of conduct.
3. Ban using inaccurate, inflated, or deceptive statements or claims in communications.
4. Fulfill account opening conditions requiring firms to collect customer information per FINRA Rule 4512 (Customer Account Information); authorize specific accounts, like options accounts (FINRA Rule 2360(b)(16)is on Diligence in Opening Accounts) and other regulatory controls concerning options.
5. Create an exhaustive supervisory system for communication methods, in-cluding red flags of likely disruptive behavior, and for keeping books and records of all firm-related business communications.
6. FINRA communications rules include the following:

   a. Rule 2210: Public communications
   b. Rule 2211: Public communications concerning variable Life insur-ance and variable annuities
   c. Rule 2212: Utilization of rankings of investment company in retail communications
   d. Rule 2213: Necessities for using bond mutual fund volatility ratings
   e. Rule 2214: Requirements for investment analysis tools use
   f. Rule 2215: Public communications regarding securities futures
   g. Rule 2216: Public communications regarding collateralized mortgage obligations
   h. Rule 2220: Options Communications

Specific Provisions Under FINRA 2210

1. Appraisal and authorization of Rule 2210(b) states that all public com-munications must meet the approval of a registered principal before dissemination.
2. Scope benchmarks of Rule 2210(d) illuminate the content standards re-garding the requirements for furnishing investors with congruous and non-misleading information, such as excessive assertions. All statements must be factual and present the risks and benefits satisfactorily.

3. Banned content of Rule 2210(d)(1) discusses strictly restricted content under Rule 2210, including warranties of future performance, dishonest testimonials, and projections of investment outcomes.

Required Disclosures

The following topics are relevant for studying:

1. Types of accounts, such as prime brokerage, delivery versus payment/receive versus payment (DVP/RVP), pattern day trading,
2. Account registration types such as community property, sole proprietorship, partnership, unincorporated associations, and tenants in common (TIC)
3. Conditions for opening customer accounts
4. Retirement plans and other accounts that are tax-advantaged
5. Rollovers, eligibility, distribution strategies, transfers, and taxations such as distribution options, taxation of distribution at retirement, age restrictions for distributions, permissible investments, and types of allowable contributions
6. Employer-sponsored plans and ERISA, including defined benefit, profit-sharing, stock options, and stock purchase, 457, and non-qualified deferred compensation programs
7. Wealth events such as inheritance
8. Internal transfers and account registration modifications

Concerning Rules and Regulations

Rule 2273 requires the recruiting firm to deliver a FINRA-created Educational Communication (http://www.finra.org/industry/broker-recruitment-notice) to former customers that emphasize the essential features concerning the transfer of assets to the broker's recruiting firm and the direct and indirect impacts of such a transfer.

Representatives who quit their original firm to join another one may try to attract their clients from the previous firm to the new recruiting firm. They may contact former clients and underline the advantages of shifting their assets to the recruitment company and keeping their connection with the representative.

In this case, the previous customer's trust and experience with the representative may be one of the most crucial factors in deciding to transfer assets to the recruitment business. Former clients may not know other key variables to consider when transferring assets to the recruitment agency, such as direct charges.

Rule 2360 for day-trading accounts is superseded by rule 2130.

1. No member advertising a day-trading strategy, directly or indirectly, may create an account for a non-institutional client without first providing the risk disclosure statement in Rule 2270 and has one of the following:

   a. The member must approve a customer's account for a day-trading strategy per procedure and keep a record of the process.
   b. The member must obtain a written agreement from the customer stating that they do not intend to use the account for day trading unless they know the customer intends to do so.

2. A member must reasonably believe a customer's day-trading strategy is suitable before approval. The member should use reasonable efforts to obtain the customer's key facts, including

   a. Investment purposes
   b. Experience and knowledge in investment and trading
   c. Financial circumstances
   d. Tax situation
   e. Employment
   f. Spousal position and dependents
   g. Age

3. If a member promoting a day-trading strategy opens an account for a non-institutional customer, trusting a written agreement from the customer under paragraph (a)(2) and then knows the customer is using the account for a day-trading strategy, the member must soon approve the account per paragraph (a)(1), no later than 10 days after the event.
4. The member must preserve all records/written statements under this Rule per Rule 4511.
5. Explanation of terms:

a. "Day-trading strategy" is a general trading method of regular communication of intra-day orders by a customer. It helps purchase and sell transactions within the same security or securities.

b. "Non-institutional customer" does not qualify as an "institutional account" under Rule 4512(c).

The new rule 2270 on risks of day trading states that (a) excluding as stated in paragraph (b), no member fostering a day-trading strategy, explicitly or implicitly, can initiate an account for/on behalf of a non-institutional customer without first providing the disclosure statement to each customer in paper or electronic form (a). Additionally, any member offering a day-trading method must prominently display the disclosure statement on their website.

Day trading is risky. Someone with minimal money, investing or trading expertise, and low-risk tolerance should avoid it. One can expect to lose all one's money. Avoid using retirement assets, student loans, second mortgages, emergency reserves, money for education, residence, or living costs to support day trading. An investment of less than $50,000 may considerably reduce a day trader's return potential. However, an investment of $50,000 or more does not guarantee success. It requires the following considerations:

1. Discretion concerning big profits.
2. Knowledge of securities markets and a firm's operations is required.
3. Day trading on margin or short selling may lead to losses exceeding the initial investment.
4. Day trading is competitive and requires fees.

FINRA Rule 5160 (SEC) discusses the disclosure of price and concessions in selling agreements. It states that selling syndicate/group agreements must:

1. Show the price of securities to the public or the method for determining the prices.
2. Declare to whom and what conditions may grant discounts.

FINRA Rule 4512 protects seniors against financial abuse. Under FINRA Rule 4512, broker-dealers must implement the following actions:

1. Collect and record client information, including name, address, phone

number, date of birth, work position, occupation, and any employer or financial institution with whom they have an account.

2. Understand clients' investing objectives and other information to provide appropriate recommendations.

3. Record clients' investment experience, financial condition, and risk tolerance. Brokerage companies must try to add a "trusted contact" feature to customer accounts.

4. Update trusted contact information for accounts subject to Exchange Act Rule 17a-3 under Rule 4512. Under FINRA Rule 4512(c) and Exchange Act Rule 17a-3(a)(17), members must make adequate efforts to acquire and update trusted contact names and information (Conduct Rules, n.d.).

FINRA Rule 4514 on approval records for negotiable instruments drawn from a client's account mandates:

1. A firm or its members must get a client's express written approval before receiving from the customer or submitting for payment a *negotiable instrument* on the customer's checking, savings, share, or similar account. A signed negotiable instrument, a codified I Owe You (IOU), offers payment to a specific person or assignee. It is a transferable, signed document that pledges to pay the bearer money later or on demand.

2. Firms must maintain this written authorization for three years after the authorization expires when the customer's signature is absent on the negotiable instrument.

FINRA rule 4515 on authorization and recording account name or designation changes states:

1. The order forms/similar transaction records must show clients' account names/designations before executing the client's order.

2. The documents must address the authorization and documentation processes for alterations in these account names/designations.

3. Direct client information about the *essential facts* for approving the change. It must be in writing and maintained for time and accessibility under SEA Rule 17a-4(b).

4. Any pre-trade alteration requires clearance and documentation.

CBOE rule 9.1 mandates specific clauses in its Chapter XI for doing trade with the public. It states Individual Trading Permit Holders (TPH) cannot do business with the public. An authorized application on a regulated form by the Exchange allows a TPH organization to do business with the public. TPH organizations must fulfill general standards in this chapter and net capital requirements in Chapter XIII of the Rules to do business with the public. Unsatisfied requirements are cause to revoke approval.

Internal Revenue Code Section 219 specifies Individual Retirement Arrangements (IRAs) regulations. It has the following provisions:

1. (a) On allocation of tax deduction states for an individual, a deduction of an amount equivalent to the eligible retirement contributions of the individual for the taxable year is allowed.
2. (b) Maximum amount of deduction.
3. (c) Kay Bailey Hutchison Spousal IRA
4. (d) Miscellaneous restrictions and constraints
5. (e) Qualified retirement subsidy
6. (f) Miscellaneous depictions and select rules
7. (g) Cap on lessening for active parties in specific pension plans

In this provision, "**compensation**" includes money earned (401(c)(2)). Deferred compensation and pensions/annuity are not considered remuneration. The phrase "compensation" includes differential wage payments (section 3401(h)(2)). Paying a person for graduate or postdoctoral education is considered "compensation" if it is part of their gross income.

Married individuals: The maximum deduction under paragraph (b) must be determined individually for each person, not considering community property rules.

Section 415 of the Internal Revenue Code mandates a cap on dollars for benefits and grants under qualified retirement plans. Section 415(d) mandates that the Secretary of the Treasury yearly revise these limits for cost-of-living increases. It impacts other restrictions concerning deferred compensation plans under section 415. Under section 415(d), the adjustments must occur under adjustment processes akin to those used to modify benefit amounts under section 215(i)(2)(A) of the Social Security Act.

The highest employee contributions are governed by section 402(g), but the general contributions from all sources are defined by section 415.3, which includes worker deferrals, employer matching, and profit-sharing contributions.

The 415 cap for 401(k) plans is $66,000 for 2023 and $69,000 for 2024. Workers may provide up to $22,500 in 2023 and $23,000 in 2024. Contributions are deemed to be annual additions. An employer can contribute more than an individual to a 401(k). However, most employers match only up to 3% to 5% of employee contributions.

The IRS enables 50-year-olds to make yearly catch-up contributions exceeding 402(g) and 415 restrictions to promote retirement savings. As these contributions are specified individually in IRC code 414(v), they are not considered yearly additions under section 415. In a plan audit, permissible catch-up contributions are not subject to the 415 limit test. The 2023 401(k) catch-up contribution is $7,500. The tax amount stays the same in 2024. Only workers who have topped their salary-deferral contributions may make catch-up contributions. Plan members 50 and older may now make a maximum employee contribution of $30,500 in 2024 and a maximum yearly contribution of $76,500 in the same year. A 415 limit violation implies exceeding the IRS contribution limit. The IRS sets and publishes these values yearly after inflation. The maximum 401(k) or equivalent plan contribution in 2023 is $22,500. This rises to $23,000 in 2024. Crossing these limitations means addressing a 415 violation. Unresolved excess contributions may result in fines and costs (Boyte-White, 2023).

A qualified tuition program (QTP)/ 529 plan is a program by a state or an agency or instrumentality of a state, permitting a contributor to prepay a beneficiary's eligible higher education payments. QTP allows contributors to prepay or contribute to an account for a beneficiary's higher education costs at an approved educational institution/contribute to an account for the purpose. Eligible educational institutions may also create and operate QTPs to prepay beneficiaries' qualified higher education fees.

Qualified higher education expenditures include money that the designated beneficiary needs to enroll or attend any college, university, vocational school, or other postsecondary educational institution approved for Department of Education student aid. Qualified higher education expenses include tuition at an elementary or secondary public, private, or religious school, from kindergarten to grade 12, for $10,000 per year from all of the assigned beneficiary's QTPs. They also cover fees, educational materials, and tools for apprenticeship programs under the Secretary of Labor.

QTP contributions for beneficiaries are limited to their eligible higher education expenditures. QTP contributions aren't tax-deductible.

1. Tax-free accumulation of earnings.

2. The recipient doesn't have to report QTP profits as income.
3. Distributions are tax-free when used for eligible higher education expenditures (including primary or secondary public, private, or religious school tuition). A part of a payout is taxable if it exceeds the beneficiary's eligible higher education expenditures, including primary or secondary public, private, or religious school tuition.
4. Withdrawals might pay student loan principal or interest for a beneficiary or sibling. Individuals may only receive $10,000 in debt payback distributions. The student loan interest deduction doesn't apply to these funds.

The IRC plan 530 or Coverdell education savings account (ESA) establishes a trust to fund a designated beneficiary's qualified higher education. It is a tax-exempt trust/custodial account managed in the United States. While opening an account, the trust must be identified as a Coverdell ESA, and the nominated beneficiary must be under age 18 or a special needs individual.

The late Senator Paul Coverdell was the primary Senate advocate. A trust or custodian handles Coverdell ESAs, while a beneficiary gets dividends. The trust or custodian establishes and oversees ESA funds for students under 18. The custodian and recipient don't possess account funds unless they are the same person. The beneficiary must receive all ESA money before turning 30, although the custodian may identify a new beneficiary to retain the account.

Coverdell ESAs invest independently. Savings and checking accounts are cash-only and insured, whereas ESAs may store stocks, bonds, real estate funds, and mutual funds. No insurance covers these securities. ESA funds fluctuate with the value of the assets maintained in the account. Any investment firm that offers a broad selection of assets can set up Coverdell ESAs for their clients. Only the institution's investing options may limit options.

Coverdell ESA funds are tax-deferred. This exempts account securities' appreciation, interest, and profits from capital gains and income taxes. Qualified ESA payouts and contributions are tax-free and not earnings to the recipient. The recipient pays conventional income taxes on ESA distributions exceeding their permitted yearly expenses. Excess distributions from dispersing the account's assets after the recipient reaches 30 are taxed as regular income.

FINRA Suitability Rule

FINRA Rule 2111 is about general suitability obligations. FINRA Rule 2111 does not involve guidance concerning SEA Rule 15l-1 (Regulation Best Interest). FINRA Rule 2111 demands that a broker-dealer partner must have sufficient reason to believe that a proposed transaction or investment strategy involving a security or securities is appropriate for the customer, according to the information gathered through the due diligence of the firm or associated member to determine the customer's investment profile. Customer investment profiles often comprise age, previous investments, financial condition and requirements, tax status, investment goals, investment knowledge, investment timeline, liquidity requirements, and willingness to take risks. The regulation specifically includes securities investing methods, including "hold" proposals. Additionally, the guideline specifies three main suitability options: reasonable basis, customer-specific, and quantitative appropriateness. The regulation provides a revised institutional-customer exemption (FINRA Rule 2111 (Suitability) FAQ, n.d.).

Brokers must understand the product and the customer, according to Rule 2111. **The lack of an understanding by itself transgresses the suitability rule.**

Three Obligations for Recommending Investments

FINRA Rule 2111 mandates that a firm or associated person have reasonable grounds to recommend a transaction/investment strategy involving a security(s) to a customer. A broker's "recommendation," founded on the facts and situations of a particular case, triggers the rule's application. FINRA does not define "recommendation," but it offers various guidelines for businesses and brokers to consider whether communications are recommendations. Many FINRA Regulatory Notices have addressed and applied such ideas to particular events. SEC publications, FINRA cases, and interpretative letters have further stated that a broker-dealer's use or distribution of marketing or offering materials does not usually constitute a "recommendation" under the suitability rule. The SEC and FINRA recognize that certain behaviors constitute implicit recommendations that trigger suitability responsibilities. FINRA and the SEC have determined that brokers who effect client transactions without notifying the client advise such transactions, triggering the suitability obligation. Implicit recommendations to hold securities are immune from the new rule. Thus, the "hold" counsel must be explicit.

Reasonable Basis

An action's *reasonableness* will lean on the realities and cases. Ordinarily, One may ask a customer for the information. Absent "red flags," which may indicate inaccurate information or ambiguity, may prompt a broker to rely on the customer's responses. A broker may not depend solely on a customer's responses in any of the following situations:

1. Confusing/misleading questions by the broker hampering the information-gathering process.
2. An unmistakably diminished capability was shown by the customer.
3. Red flags demonstrating inaccurate customer information.

Customer-Specific Obligation

The member firm or linked individual must do "reasonable diligence" to assess the customer's investment profile. When client information is lacking despite reasonable effort, the company must carefully consider whether it understands the consumer to evaluate the advice. Although the rule includes numerous popular investment profile characteristics, not all may apply. Suppose a business or related member legitimately concludes that certain customers or accounts do not require investigation. In that case, it can note the reasons in its processes or elsewhere rather than recommendation-by-recommendation or customer-by-customer basis documentation.

When a customer reveals information to a broker about the recommendation, the broker must evaluate that information for suitability analysis. Of the requisite information, the ones detailed in the rule specifically list are mandatory. Customer-specific information will also depend on the facts and circumstances of the particular case per the firm's discretion. A firm is not mandated to ask customers pointedly if there is anything else it should learn about them. Nevertheless, attempting to gain as much pertinent information as feasible before making recommendations is advisable.

Quantitative Suitability Obligation

It mandates that a broker with authentic or de facto authority over a customer's account must have a reasonable basis for believing that a series of recommended transactions is not unreasonable and inappropriate for the customer per their investment profile. It holds even if the recommendation is fitting when regarded separately (Suitability, n.d.).

Securities Regulations

The Securities Act of 1933 is also called the "truth in securities." It has two primary ideas:

1. Mandates that investors receive financial and other essential information regarding securities offered to the public.
2. Bans deception, misrepresentation of facts, and other scams in the securities trade.

Securities Registration

Securities registration is the best way to achieve these objectives. It leads to the disclosure of important financial information. This information helps investors, and not the government. Investors can make informed decisions about purchasing a company's securities. While the SEC mandates that the furnished information be accurate, it does not ensure it. Investors who buy securities and sustain losses have necessary recovery rights when they can prove an incomplete or wrong disclosure of critical information. Exchanges, dealers, transfer agents, brokers, and clearing agencies must register with the Commission under the Act. Registration for these organizations requires frequent disclosure document updates.

Securities sold in the US are registered. Companies must file the registration forms. Companies must file:

1. Company's assets and business descriptions
2. Security description
3. Management descriptions of the company
4. Independent accountants' certified financial descriptions

Filing with the SEC makes the registration forms available. For US domestic companies, the forms are available on the EDGAR database. Disclosure requirement compliances require scrutiny of registration statements. Some exemptions from the registration requirement:

1. Private offerings to restricted persons or institutions
2. Limited size offerings
3. Intrastate offerings
4. Municipal, state, and federal government securities

The SEC encourages capital formation for smaller firms by reducing the offering cost to the public.

The Security Exchange Act of 1934 (SEA) allowed Congress to form the Securities and Exchange Commission (SEC). The SEC has extensive jurisdiction over all securities sector matters under the Act. It involves registering, regulating, and monitoring brokerage companies, transfer agents, clearing agencies, and securities self-regulatory organizations (SROs). SROs include the New York Stock Exchange, NASDAQ Stock Market, and Chicago Board of Options. FINRA is an SRO.

The Act defines and forbids trading practices and gives the Commission disciplinary authority over regulated firms and their associates. It allows the SEC to mandate periodic reporting by publicly listed firms.

Corporate reporting involves firms with assets over $10 million and over 500 shareholders. They must submit annual and other periodic reports. EDGAR provides access to these reports.

In annual or special meetings for director elections and other company activity, the Securities Exchange Act controls transparency in materials used to collect shareholders' votes. To comply with disclosure regulations, firms must submit **proxy solicitations** to the Commission before solicitation. Both management and shareholder groups must provide all relevant information about the topics up for a vote.

Anyone buying more than 5% of a company's stocks directly or via a **tender offer** must disclose critical information under the SEA. People make this to take over a firm. Like proxy regulations, this lets shareholders make informed choices on significant company events.

Securities rules prohibit offer-related fraud, acquisition, or sale. These statutes underpin several disciplinary processes, including fraud-related **insider trading**. Insider trading involves trading securities with considerable nonpublic information without withholding or abstaining.

Trust Indenture Act of 1939 covers public-sale bonds, debentures, and notes. The trust indenture must comply with the Securities Act to sell such securities to the public.

Investment Company Act of 1940 supervises investors who obtain securities from companies, including mutual funds and trade securities. Conflicts of interest in complex systems decrease. The Act requires firms to frequently disclose their financial position and investment strategies to investors when selling shares. The Act highlights the investor disclosure of fund and investment targets, firm structure, and activity. The SEC cannot actively monitor or analyze these businesses' potential investments or activities.

Investment Advisers Act of 1940 regulates investment advisers. With few exceptions, this Act requires businesses or sole practitioners advising investors on securities investments to register with the SEC and safeguard investors. The 1996 and 2010 amendments require advisers with $100 million in assets under management or registered investment enterprises to register with the Commission.

Sarbanes-Oxley Act of 2002, passed by President Bush on July 30, 2002, was considered one of the most significant reforms of American business practices. The Act created the "Public Company Accounting Oversight Board," or PCAOB, to regulate the auditing profession and required changes to improve corporate accountability, financial reporting, and corporate and accounting fraud.

On July 21, 2010, President Barack Obama sanctioned the **Dodd-Frank Wall Street Reform and Consumer Protection Act** legislation. It was to improve the US regulatory system regarding consumer protection, trading limits, credit ratings, financial product regulation, corporate governance and disclosure, and transparency (The Laws That Govern the Securities Industry, n.d.).

Chapter Three: Investment Products, Securities, and Risk Management

The US securities industry has a range of investment products satisfying diverse risk appetites. It only validates the relevance of manifold laws and regulations shielding investors from potential fraud. This chapter discusses the types of products available, such as equities, bonds, hedge funds, municipal securities, options, mutual funds, insurance products, etc. Risk management strategies are diverse and comprise diversification, hedging, and portfolio rebalancing.

Yield Spread

The yield spread is the difference between debt instrument yields of different maturities, credit ratings, issuers, or risk categories. Subtracting one instrument's yield from the other yields a yield spread. Measuring this difference in basis points (bps) or percentage points is usual.

Yield spreads compare one yield to U.S. Treasuries, which is known as the credit spread. If the five-year Treasury bond is 5% and the 30-year is 6%, the yield spread is 1%. The historical yield spread suggests that the five-year bond should trade at roughly 1% if the 30-year bond sells at 6%, making it highly appealing at 5%.

IOUs allow a firm or government to borrow money by declaring the principal, maturity date, and interest rate (coupon). Investors earn from lending money at the interest rate.

Equities

Like stocks, equities are **company shares**. Buying stocks means purchasing equities. A shareholder owns the issuing firm based on the ratio of shares they own to the number of outstanding shares. Someone who holds 1,00 shares of a firm with 1,000 shares outstanding has a 10% claim on the company's assets and profits.

Because the law recognizes companies as legal entities, shareholders do not own them. Corporations pay taxes, may borrow, and be sued. For a company to be a "person" implies it owns its assets.

Companies borrow from purchasers when they issue bonds. Equities can also be offered while joining a firm, making one partial company owner. They don't assure a guaranteed income or a fixed interest rate—an **inherent risk**.

Equities attract investors due to their large returns. In the financial portfolio, **"equity exposure"** refers to the risk of losing money if the equities drop in value.

Traditional thinking is that young individuals can afford greater equity exposure and will demand more equities due to their potential for significant returns. As retirement approaches, stock investment grows riskier. Many senior investors switch from equities to bonds.

Its benefits are as follows:

1. Reward: A firm that rapidly rises in value might provide a significant reward for a little investment.
2. Dividends: Some shares give owners capital gains dividends, generating revenue and boosting corporate value.
3. Diversification: Mutual funds, ETFs, and index funds allow one to invest in many securities from different sectors.

4. Accessibility: Equities and their advantages are simple to invest in due to their various outlets.

Companies pay **dividends** from their earnings to shareholders. Although not guaranteed, recurring payments may be beneficial. A shareholder may reinvest dividends or accept them as income.

The difference between buying and selling shares is a **capital gain**. Long-term and short-term capital gains have distinct tax rates.

Qualified dividends are **taxed** like long-term capital gains. Equities brokers and fund companies should send **IRS Form 1099-DIV,** which details the dividends and capital gains for the year.

Corporate property is legally distinct from shareholder property, limiting responsibility for both. The court may sell all the corporation's assets if it goes bankrupt, but shareholders' assets are safe. Big shareholders cannot sell firm assets to pay creditors if they go bankrupt.

Companies sell shares (**stocks/equities**) to raise funds for

1. Clearing debt
2. Launching new product
3. Entering new markets/areas
4. Expanding/constructing facilities

Common and Preferred Stockholders

Common stockholders can attend shareholder meetings and receive dividends.

Preferred investors get more income and assets. Preferred stockholders get dividends sooner and at a set pace. Due to set dividend rates, preferred shareholders' dividends don't increase when the business profits.

Preferred shareholders acquire assets and earnings first if the company fails or liquidates. **Bondholders get a company's assets first if it fails**. Preferred shareholders precede common stockholders.

Both types include the following:

1. Growth stock: Earnings of growth stocks are faster than the market average. They rarely pay dividends. Investors buy them for capital appreciation. A start-up technology company is likely a growth stock.
2. Income stocks: these pay regular dividends or income. An accomplished utility company can be an income stock.
3. Value stocks: When growth or income stocks have a low price-to-earnings (PE) ratio, they are cheaper than stocks with a higher PE. It occurs when they are unwanted by investors for some reason. People buy value stocks thinking an overreacting market has negatively affected the stock's price, which will eventually rebound.
4. Blue-chip stocks: Shares in large, well-known companies with a robust growth history generally pay dividends and are valued by investors.

Warrants

Warrants grant the right but not an obligation to purchase or sell a security—usually an equity—at a specific price before expiry. Exercise or strike prices are the underlying security's purchase or sale price. Investors exercise **American warrants** before or on the expiration date and **European warrants** on the expiration date. Call warrants allow investors to acquire a security, while put warrants allow them to sell it.

While warrants and options are similar, there are key differences:

1. Warrants trade mostly over the counter.
2. A corporation issues warrants.
3. Investors cannot write warrants like options.
4. Warrants provide no dividends or voting rights.
5. Warrants allow investors to leverage their holdings, hedge downside risk using put warrants and long stock investments, or investigate arbitrage opportunities.
6. Hong Kong, Germany, and others offer warrants, although they are uncommon in the US.

Types of warrants include:

1. Warrant-linked bonds are **traditional warrants**. They have a reduced coupon rate. They can be detached from the bond and traded on the secondary market before expiry. Preferred stock might have a detachable warrant.
2. To execute a **wedded/wedding warrant**, the investor must relinquish the bond or preferred stock it is "wedded" to.
3. Financial entities issue **covered warrants** instead of firms. They don't issue new stock when covered warrants are used. Rather, the warrants are "covered" since the issuing institution owns or can buy the underlying shares. Unlike other warrants, they are more than equities and may be currencies, commodities, or other financial instruments.

Due to the lack of warrant listings on major exchanges and free warrant data, trading and researching warrants may be time-consuming. An exchange-listed warrant's ticker symbol can be the company's common stock with an emblematic alphanet. The Black Scholes model rates warrants. Warrants trade at a premium with time decay near expiry.

Derivative warrants **reduce (dilute) each shareholder's equity in the issuing business**. If you execute a warrant to acquire 1 share in a company with 10 outstanding shares, the number of shares outstanding will grow to 11. Others will lose a part of their firm equity while you gain control (Chen, 2023).

Rights Issue

Rights issues allow current shareholders to buy new business shares. Existing shareholders get rights in this offering. The shareholder may buy new shares at a discount on a stated future date using the rights. The company offers stockholders a discount to increase their exposure.

Features

1. A cash-strapped firm might obtain funds via a rights issue to pay off debt.
2. Shareholders may acquire fresh shares at a discount for a period.
3. A rights issue dilutes the stock price by issuing additional shares.

4. Until the new shares are available, shareholders may exchange the rights like ordinary shares.
5. Rights offerings dilute a company's net earnings by spreading it over more shares. As allocated profits dilute shares, the company's **earnings per share** (EPS) declines.

Purposes

1. For the firm:

   a. Firms most commonly offer rights to raise capital or pay debts.
   b. Healthy companies may use a rights issue to purchase a rival or develop additional facilities, which may create capital gains for the shareholder.

2. For the client:

   a. Subscribe to the right issue entirely with a profit less than the original shares due to dilution.
   b. Ignore the rights, which will dilute the investors' shareholdings.
   c. Sell the rights to others. Rights are non-transferable. These are non-renounceable privileges. The investor may acquire the shares or sell your rights to other investors or the underwriter. Renounceable rights are tradeable. After trading, rights are nil-paid. A rough estimate of the profit for nil-paid rights can be estimated.

American Depositary Receipts

US banks issue convertible American Depositary Receipts (ADR) that reflect a specific amount of shares in a foreign firm that operates in US financial markets. ADRs started in 1927 in the US. ADRs trade like stocks and pay US dollar dividends. Companies may bulk-buy overseas stocks and reissue them in the US. Over-the-counter deals are available. ADRs are listed in NASDAQ, NYSE, and AMEX ADRs.

Features

1. Brokers and dealers sell American Depositary Receipts. Brokers and dealers acquire or create ADRs in US financial markets. NASDAQ and NYSE offer already issued ADR.
2. Buying foreign firm equities on the issuer's home market and depositing them in an offshore depository bank creates a new ADR. The bank issues ADRs equivalent to the shares deposited, and the dealer/broker sells them in US financial markets. Pricing, availability, and demand determine ADR creation.
3. ADR holders get US dollar dividends. Foreign banks pay dividends in their home currencies, and dealers/brokers distribute them in US dollars after currency translation expenses and foreign taxes.
4. US investors can invest in overseas companies without worrying about currency exchange rates. US banks that deal with ADRs instruct overseas firms to provide financial information, which investors use to assess their financial health.

Types

1. Sponsored ADRs: An arrangement with a US depositary bank allows a foreign business to offer its shares in US markets via a sponsored ADR. The US bank keeps records, sells and distributes shares, and distributes dividends. Sponsored ADRs may trade on US exchanges.

    a. Level I: International corporations who don't qualify for other levels or don't want their equities listed on US marketplaces may choose the lowest sponsored ADR level, I. Over-the-counter Level I ADRs need the least SEC reporting. Corporations do not report yearly/regularly like public firms. *Level I issuers must list domestically.* Level I may become Level II when the company sells on US exchanges.

    b. Level II: Level II ADRs have more SEC restrictions than Level I, but the firm can trade more on US stock exchanges. The business must register with the SEC and submit Form-20-F per GAAP or IFRS standards. The counterpart of Form-10-K for US publicly listed corporations is Form 20-F. Delisting or Level I downgrading may occur if the issuer fails to cooperate.

    c. Level III: Foreign companies may sponsor Level III, the highest and most coveted. International firms may now publicly offer ADRs on the US market to obtain funds from American investors. SEC rules are more rigid for Level III ADRs. The business must submit Form F-1 (prospectus) and Form 20-F (annual reports). The SEC must receive Form 6-K, which includes shareholder documents disseminated in the issuer's home country. Some examples include Vodafone, Petrobras, etc.

2. Non-sponsored ADRs: Brokers produce non-sponsored ADRs without the foreign firm issuing the shares. They are **traded over-the-counter** in the US market without SEC registration. Before 2008, ADR brokers and dealers had to file a formal application to trade in the US. The 2008 SEC amendment exempted foreign issuers under specific regulations.

Real Estate Investment Trust

A real estate investment trust (REIT) is a business that holds, operates, or funds income-generating real estate. It attracts investors to gain market capital. Congress founded REITs in 1960, modifying the Cigar Excise Tax Extension. The provision authorizes investors to purchase shares in **commercial** real estate portfolios.

Features

1. REITs are businesses that own, operate, or fund income-producing assets.
2. Major securities exchanges publicly traded REITs as stocks.
3. REITs typically trade in considerable volume.
4. Investors get a regular income from REITs but limited capital gain.
5. Unlike physical assets, REITs are highly liquid.
6. Standard REIT investments include housing complexes, cell towers, data centers, hotels, medical facilities, etc.

Criteria

REIT companies must satisfy these criteria per the Internal Revenue Code (IRC):

1. Invest 75% of assets in real estate, cash, or US Treasuries.
2. Generate at least 75% of the revenue from rentals, mortgage interest, or real estate sales.
3. Annually distribute 90% of taxable profits as shareholder dividends.
4. It is a corporation-taxable entity.
5. The board of directors or trustees manage it.
6. It has at least 100 stockholders after its first year
7. Five or fewer people hold no more than 50% of its shares.

Types

1. Equity: Holds and manages income-producing real estate.
2. Mortgage: Possess mortgages on real estate.
3. Hybrid: Holds both properties and mortgages.
4. Publicly traded REITs: Listed on the national securities exchange and regulated by the SEC.
5. Public Non-Traded REITs:

   a. Registered with the SEC.
   b. Do not trade on national securities exchanges.
   c. Less liquid than publicly traded REITs.

6. Private REITs:

   a. REITs are not registered with the SEC.
   b. They do not trade on national securities exchanges.
   c. They are typically sold only to institutional investors.

Debt Securities (Bonds)

A debt security is a debt instrument bought or sold between two parties. It has well-defined basic terms, such as the notional amount, which is the borrowed amount, interest rate, and maturity and renewal dates. **Debt securities are negotiable instruments.** Their *legal possession is transferable between owners.*

The bond is the most common example. Governments and corporations sell bonds to raise money for infrastructure, expansion, or other purposes.

Government and corporate bonds, certificates of deposit (CD), municipal bonds, and preferred stock can be debt securities. Zero-coupon securities and collateralized securities issued by the Government National Mortgage Association (GNMA), such as collateralized mortgage obligations (CMOs), mortgage-backed securities (MBSs), and collateralized debt obligations (CDOs), are some examples.

The features of bonds are as follows:

- They are financial assets paying regular interest.
- The borrower must repay the principal borrowed in bonds, unlike equity securities.
- The interest rate depends on the assumed creditworthiness of the borrower.
- Investors can sell debt securities before maturity for a capital gain/loss on their initial investment.
- Bonds are common types of debt securities.

Common Terms

In bonds, one party lends money to another. Corporations may sell debt instruments to investors as **corporate bonds**. Investors lend money for a pre-fixed number of interest payments and the repayment of the principal at maturity. Corporate bond ratings vary from Aaa to C. Baa bonds are medium-grade, meaning they are neither well-protected nor poorly safeguarded. Investment-grade bonds are Baa or above.

Governments sell debt instruments to investors as **government bonds**. Investors lend money to the government for coupon payments and a return of capital at maturity.

Debt securities are **fixed-income securities** because they pay interest. Unlike equity investments, which rely on the market performance of the equity issuer, debt instruments guarantee repayment of a set interest stream and refund the principal amount at maturity. Fixed-income securities have predictable returns, unlike variable-income securities, which depend on an underlying measure like short-term interest rates. *Bonds are the most common types of fixed-income securities.*

A note, draft, acceptance bond, or other financial instrument matures when its principal is due. It also refers to the full installment loan repayment deadline. Thus, the debtor-creditor or investor-debt issuer connection terminates at the **maturity date of the debt instrument**. The instrument certificate indicates the maturity date. The investor receives their principal investment and stops receiving interest payments on maturity.

Debt instruments are any capital-raising financial tool. A legal and written document between two parties describes one party lending funds to another. The contract mentions the repayment method. Some have collaterals; most have interest rates, a payment schedule, and a maturity date.

Risks

Still, there are risks involved. Debt securities bear the risk of *issuer default*. Financial difficulties may prevent the issuer from repaying debt interest. If they go bankrupt, they may be unable to redeem their debt at maturity. In investing in bonds, a security's risk depends on its qualities. It also depends on the firm's solidity of its balance sheet and market maturity. A strong balance sheet implies enough cash, healthy assets, and reasonable debt. The three leading credit rating agencies: S&P, Moody's Corporation, and Fitch Ratings award the mature firm a better credit rating.

In line with the risk-return tradeoff, firms with better credit ratings provide lower debt securities interest rates and vice versa. As of July 2023, Moody's Seasoned Aaa corporate bond yield is 4.66%, and Seasoned Baa is 5.74%. The Aaa grade indicates a reduced perceived risk of credit default. Hence, market participants are willing to accept a lower return for these assets.

Interest rates may vary on some factors. Selling the bonds prematurely will reduce the amount of accrued interest. The investor may just get the face value of the bond/less. Investors prefer newer bonds with a higher interest rate than older ones. Selling an older bond with a lower interest rate may require a discount.

Inflation lowers purchasing power, a risk for investors receiving a fixed interest rate.

Liquidity risk involves investors unable to find a market for the bond, prohibiting them from purchasing or selling.

Call risk occurs when a bond issuer retires a bond before its maturity date. It happens when interest rates for a home loan fall and a homeowner refinances a mortgage to avail of the lower interest rates.

Equity vs. Bonds

Equity securities have a claim on the corporation's earnings and assets. If the company gains, the investor gains, and vice versa. Equity does not have a specified duration or guarantee dividend amounts. The firm determines dividends based on its performance. Thus, without a dividend distribution plan, equity returns are unknown and risky. While selling the shares to another party, the investor receives the shares' market value, which can result in capital gain/loss.

Debt securities are investments in debt instruments the investor loans to the borrower. Its prefixed terms for loan repayments and interest return, and yield-to-maturity (YTM) ensure predicting an investor's income. The investor has no claims on the company's earnings/assets; the claim is on the principal amount and interest accrued.

Features of Debt Security

1. Debt securities must have an *issue date* and an *issue price* when first issued to the investors for buying.
2. Issuers pay an interest rate and *coupon rate*. The coupon rate may remain

fixed throughout the security's lifespan or change with inflation and economic circumstances.

3. The issuer must repay the principal at the stated value and the outstanding interest by the security's mature date. Term lengths determine the cost and interest rate. Investors can demand higher returns for longer investment terms. It classifies debt securities as follows:

   a. Short-term securities mature in less than a year.
   b. Medium-term securities mature in 1-3 years.
   c. Long-term securities mature in three or more years.

4. YTM measures the yearly rate of return an investor may expect to earn if they hold the debt to maturity. It compares bonds with identical maturity dates based on coupon payments, purchase price, and face value.

Types of Bonds

The three main types are as follows:

US Treasuries

The Treasury Department issues US Treasuries for the government. They are secure and popular investments because the US government backs them. US Treasury debt types:

1. Treasury Bills: Short-term securities maturing in days to 52 weeks
2. Notes: Securities maturing in 10 years
3. Bonds: Securities mature in 30 years and pay interest every six months.

Treasury Inflation-Protected Securities (notes and bonds) modify principal depending on the Consumer Price Index.

Municipal Bonds

Also called munis, they include government bonds such as states, municipalities, and counties.

1. General obligation bonds: Government bonds get the backing of general revenue or specific levies like property tax. State and municipal restrictions affect payment sources and priority for general obligation bond issuers. Local government general obligation bonds typically deal with property taxes, but state-issued bonds need the issuer's full faith, credit, and, usually, their taxing power.
2. Revenue bonds: Project profits like highway tolls or leasing fees replace taxes on these bonds. Revenue bonds may be "non-recourse," preventing bondholders from claiming the income source if the stream ends.
3. Conduit bonds: Private non-profit hospitals and universities may issue municipal bonds via municipalities. "Conduit" borrowers repay bond interest and principal to the issuer. If the conduit borrower fails, the issuer seldom pays bonds.

Corporate Bonds

Private and public corporations issue corporate bonds as debt securities.

1. Investment grade have a higher credit rating than high-yield corporate bonds. They have less credit risk.
2. High-yield has a lower credit rating with more credit risk than investment-grade bonds. Thus, they compensate with higher interest rates.

Specific Debt Security Types

1. Mortgage bonds
2. Equipment trust certificates
3. Collateral trust bonds
4. Debentures
5. Subordinated debentures

6. Convertible debentures
7. Junk bonds

Mortgage Bonds

A mortgage or pool of mortgages on real estate and equipment guarantees the mortgage bond. Its features are:

1. The value of the real estate supports mortgage bonds.
2. Mortgage bondholders may sell the actual asset to cover defaults.
3. Mortgage bonds offer a lower return than corporate bonds since they are safer.

After a mortgage-financed property purchase, the financier rarely retains the mortgage. Instead, it sells the mortgage to an investment bank or government-sponsored enterprise (GSE) on the secondary market. This company offers mortgage-backed bonds, pooling them with other loans/issue bonds called **securitization**.

The interest component of homeowners' mortgage payments pays the mortgage bond yield. Mortgage bonds are secure and dependable income-producing securities provided most homeowners in the mortgage pool pay their mortgages. Lessees don't pay property taxes since they don't own the asset and get tax benefits. It may change if the trust transfers ownership to the lessee. If a bankrupt or insolvent corporation fails on its debt, Equipment Trust Certificates (ETC) allow the trust to retrieve the asset.

However, the financial crisis of 2000 shifted market attention from investing in subprime mortgages, which caused a crisis leading to a loss of millions of dollars in mortgage bonds.

Equipment Trust Certificate (ETC)

An ETC is a financial instrument that lets a corporation possess and utilize an equipment/asset and pay for it over time. Equipment or tangible assets guarantee the debt issue. Issue holders have the equipment title in trust for this period. Airline ETCs are frequent for aircraft purchases. Its features are:

1. An equipment trust certificate is a debt instrument that lets an entity utilize an asset while paying for it in installments.
2. Investors fund a trust by purchasing certificates to acquire assets they lease to firms.
3. The business receives the asset's title after paying off the loan.

Enhanced Equipment Trust Certificates (EETC)

Northwest Airlines pioneered EETC aircraft financing in 1999. Pass-through trusts are special purpose vehicles (SPEs) that generate and administer EETCs. SPEs let borrowers combine equipment purchases under a single debt security. The trust creates debt, stores it, and pays investors who hold the certificate while the borrower leases the assets.

The SEC and Financial Accounting Standard Board (FASB) have questioned EETCS' accounting status as an independent economic entity. SPEs allow borrowers to offload their debt commitments from their balance sheets. Thus, their financial statements frequently don't reveal their borrowings. Financial Interpretation Notice (FIN) 46 of FASB specifies when corporations should merge or present off-balance sheet assets and liabilities for these vehicles.

Collateral Trust Bond

A company deposits stocks, bonds, or other assets with a trustee to obtain a collateral trust bond. *It is a secured bond.* Companies seek strategies to lower their borrowing costs, one of which is to issue debt with low interest rates. To do this, they secure the bond with the collateral's security.

Holding firms commonly issue these bonds since they have fewer assets to offer. Instead, holding corporations control subsidiaries by owning shares in them, offering a collateral trust bond against subsidiary securities. A trustee manages the bondholders' collateralized securities. These securities offer voting rights to the corporate issuer even if the trustee holds the pledged assets.

At bond issuance, the collateral must have a market value at least equivalent to the bonds. Regularly checking the collateral's value regularly ensures it meets the promised value. If the collateral value drops below the agreed-upon minimum, the issuer must provide more securities or cash as collateral. Although safer than unsecured bonds, this kind yields less and pays less.

If a corporation is insolvent or defaults on debt payments, it may sell its assets. The bondholders get paid back first. The holders of secured bonds get reimbursed before the holders of unsecured bonds.

Debentures

A debenture is an unsecured bond in the US, although secured by company assets in the UK. In some countries, the terms are convertible. It is the most common type of bond, such as a US Treasury bond and a US Treasury bill. Not being tied to collateral, the value of a debenture rests on the reputation and trustworthiness of the issuer. Its essential features are as follows:

1. A debenture is an unsecured debt instrument with no collateral backing.
2. Its usual term is greater than 10 years.
3. Some debentures can change to equity shares; some cannot.
4. Debentures provide coupon payments, which are regular interest payments. Companies set coupon rates, which can be fixed or variable. Typically, tying a benchmark such as the 10-year Treasury bond yield to the coupon rate can make it a floating rate. It will change with the benchmark changes.
5. Like other bonds, an indenture documents debentures. Indentures are *binding contracts* between bond issuers and bondholders. It describes debt offering elements, including maturity date, interest or coupon payment schedule, interest calculation technique, etc.
6. Governments usually issue bonds with a maturity period longer than 10 years. The government issuer backs these low-risk government bonds.
7. Corporations borrow long-term via debentures. They rely on the company's financial stability and credibility.
8. Interest-bearing debt instruments are redeemable on a specific date. Companies usually pay such planned debt interest before stock dividends.

Lower interest rates and more extended payback deadlines than other loans and debt instruments benefit corporations.

Debenture Types

Registered debentures have the name of the issuer. Transferring or selling such assets requires a clearing institution to notify the issuer of ownership changes so they can pay interest to the right bondholder. *Bearer debentures* are not issuer-registered. Debenture holders (bearers) receive interest by holding the bond.

Redeemable debentures specify the issuer's repayment conditions and deadline. However, *irredeemable debentures* do not require the issuer to fully return by a specific date. Thus, irredeemable debentures are also known as *perpetual debentures*.

Convertible debentures can turn into equity shares of the issuing company after a period. These hybrid financial products combine debt and equity advantages. These are fixed-rate loans with fixed interest. Debenture holders may maintain the debt till maturity and receive interest payments or convert it into equity shares. Convertible debentures appeal to investors who expect the company's stock to grow. Convertible debentures pay a lower interest rate than comparable fixed-rate investments. Therefore, converting to equity costs money.

Traditional *nonconvertible debentures* do not convert into company stock. Investors get a higher interest rate than convertible debentures to compensate for the absence of conversion. Hence, the maturity date is important in nonconvertible debentures. The corporation must repay debenture holders at this date. The corporation might choose repayment methods. The issuer usually pays a lump sum payment at debt maturity as capital redemption. The corporation may also employ a redemption reserve to pay a particular amount each year until a full refund at maturity.

Credit Ratings and Junk Debentures

Credit-rating firms assess business and government debt. These organizations explain debt investment concerns to the investors. Investors' interest rates depend on the company's and debenture's credit ratings.

Credit rating companies like Standard & Poor's issue letter grades to indicate the creditworthiness of a corporation. S&P's grade covers a range of scales from AAA for exceptional to C and D for lowest ratings. Any debt instrument below BB is speculative.

High-yield corporate bonds (junk bonds) attract investors owing to their greater yields than investment-grade securities. However, these bonds offer higher yields due to increased credit risks and default rates. Three major crises have hit the junk bond market: the 1980s savings & loan crisis, the dot-com bubble of the early 2000, and the 2008 financial crisis.

Bonds are junk when the debt issuer is more prone to default. Standard & Poor's rates junk bonds BB[+] or lower and Moody's Ba[1]. Their lower credit rating explains why junk bonds must provide higher interest rates to entice investors.

The following table explains the risk ratings (Everything You Need to Know About Junk Bonds, 2023).

Moody Bond Ratings	Standard & Poor's Bond Ratings	Grade	Risk
Aaa	AAA	Investment	Lowest risk
Aa	AA	Investment	Low risk
A	A	Investment	Low risk
Baa	BBB	Investment	Medium risk
Ba, B	BB, B	Junk	High risk
Caa/Ca/C	CCC/CC/C	Junk	Highest risk
C	D	Junk	In default

Junk bond rates are typically 4% to 6% higher than Treasury bonds. If the yield spread falls below 4%, junk bonds may not be worthwhile. Until July 31, 2023, the spread was 3.79%.

In contrast, low-risk to medium-risk lenders offer *investment-grade bonds*. Bond ratings for investment-grade debt vary from AAA to BBB. These high-rated bonds offer lower interest. Investors seeking complete safety will purchase them. US bonds are the benchmark for investment-grade bonds since the country has never defaulted.

Investors classify junk bonds into two groups:

Because of financial worries, *fallen angels* are junk bonds that were formerly investment grade. Their lowered gradation to junk bond status is due to concerns regarding their issuers' financial position.

In contrast to fallen angels, *the rising stars* are gaining prosperity. The bond issuers are improving financially. Although they are still junk, if everything works well, they might become investment-grade.

High-yield bond funds are an alternative for junk bond investors apprehensive about choosing them individually.

Subordinated Debenture

A subordinated debenture is an unsecured bond or debt. It ranks below senior loans or securities regarding claims on assets or profits. Subordinated debentures are junior securities. Subordinated creditors receive payments after senior bondholders in the event of borrower failure. It is a long-term liability on the balance sheet after unsubordinated debt and is riskier in comparison.

In 1999, the Federal Reserve advised banks to issue subordinated debt to reduce risk. It would necessitate risk profiling, revealing a bank's finances and activities after the expiration of the Glass-Steagall Act. Its attractions are:

- Lenders pay subordinated debt before equity despite its riskier nature.
- Subordinated debt bondholders get a higher interest rate to offset the risk of default.
- Many firms issue subordinated debt, but the banking sector deserves particular mention. Banks prefer such debt instruments because interest is tax-deductible.
- Mutual savings banks may use subordinated debt to achieve Tier 2 capital requirements.

Difference Between Senior Debt and Subordinate Debt

1. Payment of senior debt precedes subordinate debt payment if a company liquidates or declares bankruptcy.
2. Senior debt is the highest priority and lowest risk. Low-interest rates are typical for this loan. Lower repayment priority raises interest rates on subordinated debt.

Banks fund senior debt. Banks can afford a lower rate because of their low-cost deposit and savings account funding. Therefore, they assume the lower-risk senior position in the repayment sequence. Regulators advise banks to have low-risk lending portfolios.

Subordinated debt includes mezzanine debt that also comprises an investment. Asset-backed securities are subordinate to senior tranches. Loans, leases, credit card debt, royalties, and receivables qualify as assets for asset-backed securities. Tranches are loans or securities that separate risk or group features to appeal to various investors.

Debenture Advantages

1. Investors get a regular coupon rate on debentures.
2. The ability to convert convertible debentures to equity shares after a particular period is attractive.
3. Debenture holders get payment before common stockholders in case of company insolvency.

Debenture Disadvantages

1. In increasing interest rate settings, fixed-rate debentures may involve interest rate risk. This risk model involves investors holding fixed-rate loans amid increasing interest rates. These investors may experience lower debt returns than other assets paying the market rate. Debenture holders get a reduced yield.

2. The underlying issuer's financial viability affects default risk; hence, creditworthiness matters.
3. Debentures may be inflationary if the coupon paid does not keep pace with the inflation rate.

Municipal Securities

Local, county, and state governments issue municipal bonds, a type of debt security. They commonly pay for capital expenditures, such as constructing roads, bridges, or schools.

Municipal bonds act like loans. The bondholders are creditors. Bondholders/investors receive interest on their principal balance in exchange for borrowed capital. Repayment of the principal occurs at the maturity date. Municipal bonds are often tax exempted. Hence, they are attractive to people in higher income tax brackets. Brokers usually get a markup on the bond's cost to the company. The confirmation statement may show this markup and any commissions (Municipal bonds, n.d.).

Municipal bonds or munis can be general obligation and revenue bonds. A non-profit organization, a private-sector corporation, or another public entity can issue a muni. General obligation (GO) munis gather tax from a project, or from property tax, which ensures cash flows. Revenue munis provide cash flows that come from the project itself. The coupon rate is typically lower because of tax exemption and a steady stream of assured returns.

Although the interest on most munis are exempt from federal taxes, this is not always the case. The source of interest and principal repayments characterizes municipal bonds. Distinct bond structures provide unique benefits, hazards, and tax implications. Taxes may sometimes apply to municipal bond income. For instance, a municipality may issue a bond without federal tax exemption, subjecting the revenue to federal taxes.

Conduit Issuer

A conduit issuer is generally a government body that issues municipal securities to obtain finance for revenue-generating projects. A third party acts as the "conduit borrower" and invests the money in a public benefit initiative. Outside investors pledging to fund the project or the conduit borrower's credit usually support conduit finance. If a project fails and the security defaults, the borrower faces financial consequences.

Industrial development revenue bonds (IDRBs), housing revenue bonds (single-family and multifamily), and private activity bonds are conduit financing options. Most conduit-issued securities fund public projects (airports, docks, sewage systems) or targeted populations (students, low-income house purchasers, veterans). The conduit issuer collects taxes, fees, and earnings from the borrower and pays bondholders but is typically not liable for repayment. The borrowing organization must return bond interest and principal unless a written agreement indicates otherwise. Thus, A local nonprofit organization that utilizes conduit financing to create a new facility must repay the loan, not the conduit issuer.

Features of Municipal Bonds

1. Municipal bonds have *lower default risk* than corporate bonds. Consumer preferences and economic downturns affect revenue bonds more than GO bonds. It is understandable because water, sanitation, and other basic utilities provide more reliable revenue sources than a park's rentable pavilion.
2. A municipal bond is a *fixed-income security*. Its market prices vary with interest rate changes. Bond prices fall when rates rise; when interest rates fall, bond prices rise.
3. *A bond with a longer maturity is more vulnerable to interest rate movements*, creating significant income variations for municipal bond investors. Most municipal bonds are illiquid, so investors requiring cash must sell other assets.
4. The issuer may redeem many municipal bonds having *call provisions* before maturity. Municipal bond issuers call bonds as interest rates decline and reissue them at reduced rates. Calling a bond means losing interest income and reinvesting in a lower-return bond.
5. Local governments usually issue $5,000 bonds. Investors may buy

municipal bond fractions in exchange-traded funds (ETFs) and mutual funds. The length of the bonds vary from two to thirty years.

Risk of Munis

1. Call risk: If interest rates fall, an issuer may repay a bond before its maturity date. Stable or rising interest rates reduce such risks. Many municipal bonds are "callable." Investors who intend to hold them to maturity should examine the call clauses before buying.
2. Credit risk: Financial problems of the bond issuer may hinder paying interest and principal in full, known as default.
3. Interest rate risk: Par value is a bond's face value. Investors get the par value and interest at a fixed or adjustable rate if they hold bonds until maturity. Since the bond's market price will vary with interest rates, its market value may be greater or less than its par value. Investors who sell a low-fixed-rate municipal bond before maturity may lose money if prices rise in the current US scenario of low interest rates.
4. Inflation risk: It affects bond prices and purchasing capacity.
5. Liquidity risk: Investors may not locate an active municipal bond market, preventing them from purchasing or selling at a specific price when they want. Many investors hold municipal bonds rather than trade them. Hence, the market may be less liquid for them. The same bond may have a different ask price.

Municipal Securities Rulemaking Board

The Municipal Securities Rulemaking Board, or MSRB, is a self-regulatory entity. It promotes a fair and efficient municipal securities market to safeguard investors, state and local governments, and other municipal organizations and protect the public interest. MSRB regulates municipal securities businesses, banks, and advisers to accomplish this goal. The MSRB's Electronic Municipal Market Access (EMMA) website gives free public access to municipal securities documents and data.

The EMMA promotes market transparency to safeguard market participants. The MSRB delivers impartial municipal market research, educates and engages stakeholders, and leads on significant issues. Congress charters the MSRB. A board of directors with a majority of public members and representatives of regulated entities governs the organization. The Securities and Exchange Commission oversees the MSRB, which designated the EMMA website as the official municipal securities disclosure repository in 2009. The EMMA website provides free public access to papers and data to promote municipal securities market transparency.

- Specific Municipal Securities Information

    o   Municipal bond prospectuses
    o   Historical bond trade prices, yields, and other data
    o   Financial disclosures from the bond issuer
    o   Continuing disclosures concerning bond events
    o   Information on 529 savings schemes, of the Stephen A. Beck, Jr Achieving a Better Life Experience Act of 2014 (ABLE) programs

- Market-Wide Information

    o   Third-party yield curves and indices
    o   Calendar of municipal securities offerings
    o   Schedule of economic data and events that may affect municipal bonds.
    o   Market data on trading trends and top securities

ABLE established tax-advantaged saving programs under Section 529A of the Internal Revenue Code to assist blind or disabled individuals to maintain their healthiness, autonomy, and quality of life. Eligible individuals and families may save tax-deferred funds for qualified disability expenditures up to certain limits while remaining eligible for Social Security Income (SSI) and other government programs under ABLE. ABLE account balances exceeding $100,000 will suspend SSI benefits but not cancel them. Other benefits, such as Medicaid, will remain.

Options

Options allow investors to profit from stock price movements without owning the shares. Because they depend on the underlying asset's price, *options are derivatives*. Option underlying assets might be stocks, ETFs, index values, debt instruments (such as bonds or index-linked notes), or foreign currencies.

Options offer the option holder the privilege, without the responsibility, to purchase or trade the underlying asset at a fixed price within a scheduled time. This price is the strike price of the option.

The seller or writer of options bears the obligation to purchase or sell if the purchaser exerts their right. Upon assignment, the seller or the writer of options must purchase or sell the underlying asset, which means the seller's brokerage company requires the seller to meet the contract's requirements.

Options spreads combine purchasing and selling options to achieve the appropriate risk-return profile. Spreads may use *vanilla options* (regular options) to take advantage of high or low volatility conditions, up or down moves, or everything in between.

In contrast, *exotic options* like barrier, Asian, and digital are sophisticated and traded over the counter. They may lower net cost or boost leverage by forming complicated structures.

Its features are:

1. Call options, or index options, allow the holder to purchase the underlying asset or its value for index options. In return for the premium the holder furnishes, an assigned seller for the call option agrees to sell the stock (or asset value) at the strike price.
2. Puts transfer the right to sell shares to the purchaser, but not the obligation. They give the seller the obligation to buy shares per contract assignment. A long put is a short position in the underlying security. The put gains value as the price of the underlying falls or they have a negative delta. Protective puts are types of insurance. It offers a price floor for investors to hedge their positions.

3. Options propose leverage. It is the ability to amplify the value or purchasing power of the premium the purchaser pays. However, leverage can have the risk of substantial losses.
4. Trading options need explicit approval from an investor's brokerage firm.
5. Before trading options, studying the firm's characteristics and risks of standardized options is essential.

Option Risks

The options market utilizes "Greeks" terms to define the risk levels of adopting an option or portfolio position. Greeks refer to variables related to Greek symbols.

Each risk variable emerges from an erroneous assumption or the connection of the option with another underlying variable. Different Greek values help traders measure options risk and manage portfolios.

Option Advantages

Options provide leverage and risk hedging. Call options allow investors to leverage their position by boosting their purchasing power. If the investor already has exposure to that firm and wishes to lessen it, they may hedge the risk by selling put options against it.

1. A call option buyer can buy assets below market price when the stock price increases.
2. Put option buyers benefit by selling shares at the strike price if the market price drops below it.
3. Option sellers earn a premium from buyers for writing options.

Option Disadvantages

Option's complexity is its main disadvantage.

1. The option seller may have to acquire the asset at a higher strike price than usual if the market declines.
2. Call option writers incur unlimited risk if the stock price increases, and they must acquire shares at a high price.
3. Option writers require an upfront payment from purchasers.

Options versus Futures

Options and futures are derivatives transactions based on an asset or security. Options contracts provide the right but not the obligation to purchase or sell the underlying. Futures have such commitments (Chen, 2023).

Trading options involves using dialects called "lingo." Some crucial terminology are as follows:

1. At-the-money (ATM)is an option whose strike price is precisely that of where the underlying is trading. ATM options have a delta of 0.50.
2. In-the-money (ITM) is an option with inherent value. It has a delta more than 0.50. The strike price of an ITM option is less than the current price of the underlying for a call. For a put, it will be above the current price.
3. Out-of-the-money (OTM) is an option with only extrinsic value: the time. It has a delta of less than 0.50. For a call, an OTM option's strike price will exceed the underlying price. For a put, it will be below the current price.
4. Premium is the price at which an investor purchases a market option.
5. The strike price is the amount at which one can purchase or sell the underlying. It is also known as the exercise price.
6. Underlying is the security that creates the option.
7. Implied volatility (IV) is the volatility of the underlying. It means how quickly and aggressively it moves. The market value of the option reveals it.
8. Exercise refers to the right of the contract owner to buy or sell an option at the strike price. The seller is considered as assigned.
9. Expiration is when the options contract expires or ceases to be. OTM options will expire valueless.

Mutual Funds and Exchange-Traded Funds (ETFs)

Derivatives

Derivatives are financial instruments that rely on the performance of an underlying asset, investment, or index. Even tiny market moves might drastically change their worth, sometimes unexpectedly. Different types of derivatives have various applications. A mutual fund or ETF prospectus explains derivative usage. Investors might ask a fund to learn how it utilizes these instruments.

Mutual funds are SEC-registered open-end investment companies that combine customer funds and invest in various securities or assets, including stocks, bonds, and short-term money-market instruments. The mutual fund employs an SEC-registered investment advisor to manage its portfolio, which includes the pooled securities and assets. Each mutual fund share reflects an investor's component of the portfolio and its income.

Mutual fund shareholders purchase and redeem shares from the mutual funds directly from the fund or via investing experts like brokers. Under the law, mutual funds must price their shares daily, usually after the closure of the main US exchanges.

A mutual fund's *net asset value* (NAV) is the per-share value of its assets minus its liabilities. Mutual funds must sell and redeem shares at the computed NAV once an investor puts a buy or redemption order. When an investor submits a buy order for mutual fund shares during the day, The purchase price won't be available until the computation of the following NAV.

ETFs are a form of investment under the class of investment products called exchange-traded products (ETPs). ETPs offer varied financial product types that expose investors to various asset classes, benchmarks, and strategies. They trade on national securities exchanges and secondary markets and are widely accessible to market investors.

Other ETPs include exchange-traded commodities funds and exchange-traded notes (ETNs).

Exchange-traded commodity funds are trusts or partnerships that hold precious metals or a portfolio of futures or derivatives contracts on commodities or currencies. ETNs are secured debt liabilities of financial organizations and trade on a securities exchange.

The performance of a reference index or benchmark determines the payment conditions for ETNs, signifying their investment aim. ETNs are risky and challenging for investors, with the potential for complete loss.

Mutual Funds and ETFs

Three main kinds of investment businesses are:

1. Open-end funds, which sell shares continuously. One can acquire and redeem it through the fund or the fund's broker. Examples include mutual funds.
2. Closed-end investment companies or funds vend a set number of shares in an initial public offering called one time and sell on a secondary market. Examples are mutual funds and some ETFs.
3. Unit Investment Trusts (UITs) offer a specific number of redeemable securities called units that end and dissolve on a scheduled date.

Mutual Funds versus ETFs

Similarities:

1. ETFs, like mutual funds, are SEC-registered investment businesses *that allow investors to invest in a fund* that trades in stocks, bonds, or a mix of these assets in exchange for an interest in the investment pool.
2. ETFs, like mutual funds, must compute their NAV daily.
3. Investment advisors registered with the SEC handle most funds and ETFs.
4. Diversifying investments among firms or industries helps reduce risk in case of loss. Investors often find diversifying via mutual funds or ETFs cheaper than through individual bonds.
5. Mutual funds and ETFs may provide modest initial and monthly purchase amounts for investors with limited cash.

6. Mutual fund shareholders may redeem their shares at the next computed NAV, subtracting any fees on any business day. ETF investors may exchange shares at market price after fees whenever the market is open. Mutual funds must pay investors for shares within seven days, although many offer earlier payments. Brokers must settle ETF and mutual fund shares they sell within two business days.

7. Mutual fund investors are responsible for paying sales charges, yearly fees, management fees, and other expenditures regardless of outcome. ETF investors must cover brokerage commissions, yearly fees, management fees, and other expenditures, irrespective of performance.

8. Investors in mutual funds and ETFs cannot directly choose the types of assets in their portfolios.

Dissimilarities:

1. Unlike mutual funds, ETFs *do not sell or redeem individual shares with ordinary investors*.

2. ETFs trade on national stock markets at market prices, which can vary from the NAV.

3. ETF sponsors contracts with one or more *authorized participants*, usually big broker-dealers. authorized participants are often the only ones who buy and redeem ETF shares. Furthermore, they can only trade in huge blocks, such as 50,000 ETF shares, called *creation units*, and often trade them for a basket of securities and assets resembling the ETF's portfolio.

4. Capital gains distributions for mutual funds and ETFs may be subject to taxes for investors. However, certain ETFs redeem profits in kind, resulting in lower taxes than mutual fund investments. ETF tax efficiency is irrelevant if investors own mutual funds or ETFs in tax-advantaged accounts like IRAs or 401(k).

5. Investors may acquire real-time stock and ETF prices from financial websites or brokers. Mutual funds calculate their NAV hours after issuance, which affects the price at which investors buy or redeem their shares.

Premium and Discount: ETFs

After receiving a block of ETF shares, an authorized participant may sell them to investors in the secondary market. An ETF share trades at a premium when its market price exceeds the value of its underlying assets. A discount occurs when an ETF share's market price is lower than its underlying assets' value. The website of an ETF or its sponsor frequently displays a history of end-of-day premiums and discounts, comparing its NAV per share to its closing market price per share.

Types of Mutual Funds and ETFs

Bond Funds

Bond funds hold bonds or debt securities as their primary investment. These funds often have greater hazards than money market funds due to their focus on yield-oriented strategies. SEC guidelines do not limit bond funds to high-quality or short-term investments, unlike money market funds. The risks and benefits of bond funds may vary significantly because of the variety of bond kinds.

Stock (Equity) Funds

Stock funds generally invest in stocks, also known as equities. Stock fund values may fluctuate rapidly. But they have traditionally outperformed alternative assets in the long run, including corporate bonds, government bonds, and treasury instruments.

Stock funds are vulnerable to investing risks, including market risk, the biggest risk for investors. Stock prices may change due to several factors, including the economy and demand for certain goods or services.

Growth Funds

Companies with strong growth potential may issue growth stocks. Buying shares in such firms may lead to enormous capital appreciation for investors. Growth stocks can be risky since issuing companies are growing. The advantages of growth funds are high returns and a hedge against inflation.

These corporations issue growth stocks with high price-to-earnings (P/E) ratios, signaling strong returns on investment. Economic booms, chronic inflation, and financial bubbles occasionally affect such enterprises, creating a spurious high P/E ratio.

P/E ratio = Market value per share / Earnings per share

Due to P/E ratio limits, investors use price-earnings to growth ratio when separating growth shares from conventional equity shares. The PEG ratio tracks a company's annual profits per share growth, its key advantage over the P/E ratio. A high PEG ratio suggests corporate success.

PEG ratio = Unit share market value / Earnings per share growth rate

Growth and Income Funds

Growth and income funds are "blend funds." They can be mutual funds, or ETFs, that serve the dual purpose of capital growth and current income from dividends or interest. Growth and income funds may invest exclusively in stocks or a combination of stocks, bonds, REITs, and other assets.

Like other mutual funds, any growth fund has a bias in its investing strategy, even though it aims for growth and income. The Dodge & Cox Balanced Fund seeks discounted value companies. Other funds may emphasize growth, income, or bonds. Some low-volatility funds exhibit higher volatility than others. For example, Vanguard Growth and Income Fund Investor Shares ("VQNPX") have volatility risk owing to stock market exposure.

Value Funds

A value investor or fund manager seeks undervalued stocks that sell for less than their inherent merits. Many firms' stock prices don't reflect their value. Their underlying value and growth potential are greater. Calculating a company's intrinsic worth involves its financials, business model, competitive position, management team, etc. In this regard, A corporation has value if its market value is less than its intrinsic value. Value Funds invest in value-oriented equities.

The following are investor requirements:

1. Endurance
2. Understanding macro trends
3. Exposure to high-growth stock
4. Long-term investments

Warren Buffett is a value investor.

Income Funds

Income funds focus on monthly or quarterly income rather than capital gains or appreciation. These funds are mutual funds or ETFs, including government, municipal, and corporate debt, preferred stock, money market instruments, and dividend-paying equities.

Balanced Funds

Balanced or asset allocation funds invest in equities, bonds, and money market instruments to limit risk while generating income and capital appreciation. These funds usually hold a fixed percentage of portfolio instruments. However, allocation varies across balanced funds. These funds aim to decrease risk by diversifying among investment categories. They have the same hazards that occur in connection with the underlying assets (Mutual Funds and ETFs, n.d.).

Money Market Funds

Money market funds (MMFs) have lower risks than other mutual funds, ETFs, and other investments. The legislation restricts their investment to high-quality, short-term investments from the US government, enterprises, and state and municipal governments. Government and retail MMFs aim to maintain a steady NAV of $1.00 per share but may see a drop if their assets underperform. Investor losses are uncommon yet probable. Temporary money market price changes may cause MMFs to fall below $1 NAV, causing "breaking the buck." If it continues, the MMF's investment income may fall short of operating costs or incur investment losses.

Types of MMF

Government Money Market Funds can invest at least 99.5% of its assets in government securities, repurchase agreements, or cash collateralized only by government securities or cash.

Retail investors can trade in Retail Money Market Funds. These operate within rules and procedures that restrict beneficial owners of the fund to investors they recognize as natural people.

Other money market funds have a variable NAV that varies with the market value of their portfolio holdings.

Advantages and Disadvantages of MMFs

The SEC regulates US MMFs. According to the rules, money funds invest in top-rated debt securities with a maturity duration of under 13 months. A weighted average maturity (WAM) of 60 days or fewer is necessary for the MMF portfolio. Its features are:

1. The WAM requirement limits the average maturity time of all investment securities to no more than 60 days, proportional to their fund portfolio weights. This maturity constraint ensures that only highly liquid securities are eligible, and it does not lock investors' money in low liquidity long-maturity instruments (Segal, 2023).
2. MMFs cannot invest more than 5% in any issuer to prevent issuer-specific risk. Government-issued securities and repurchase agreements are exempt.
3. All MMFs provide dividends based on short-term interest rates, with historically lower returns than bond or equity funds. In money market

funds, inflation risk is common. Inflation may outrun and reduce investment returns over time.

Money Market Funds versus Money Market Accounts (MMAs)

Investment fund companies underwrite MMFs. It is a type of interest-earning savings account. It does not assure the principal. Conversely, financial organizations provide MMAs. These Federal Deposit Insurance Corporation (FDIC)-insured accounts have restricted transaction advantages.

Rights of Accumulation (ROA)

Mutual funds set breakpoints and incorporate them into distribution. They usually apply to funds with a front-end sales fee but may also apply to other sales charges.

Mutual fund prospectuses must include breakpoints and eligibility conditions. When the total amount of purchased mutual funds and the already possessed amount equals a right of accumulation (ROA) by reaching a breakpoint, mutual fund shareholders get sales charge discounts. Surpassing a breakpoint saves investors money on sales charges.

Life Insurance and Annuities

Overview

Financial plans typically include life insurance. Term, whole, and universal life insurance are some of the forms. These have further variations. Of these, indexed universal life insurance is generally not a security; The SEC must register other varieties, like variable life and variable universal life insurance, which are securities. FINRA regulates investment professionals and companies that provide securities-like insurance.

Insurance products typically have specific purposes. As with other financial goods, insurance is complicated and has costs, requiring research before buying. Here are some popular life insurance types:

1. Term life insurance: Term life insurance typically gives coverage for a limited and set time. Most term policy premiums increase with age or the end of each renewal. Without a renewal, the insurance and coverage expire.
2. Whole life insurance: Whole or ordinary life insurance is permanent. It offers lifelong coverage and may construct cash value, a savings element. The insured usually pays the same premiums for the life of the insured.
3. Universal life insurance: Universal life gives lifelong coverage, insurance coverage, and flexible premium payments. Deduction of insurance and other charges reduces cash or policy account value.
4. Indexed universal life insurance: The universal life insurance bracket includes indexed universal life insurance. It tracks a specific stock index like the S&P 500 rather than letting policyholders pick what to invest in.
5. Variable life insurance: Variable life insurance has set premiums and a minimum death benefit. Unlike whole life insurance, its cash value is in securities. The policyholder may pick among the policy's investments. However, the policy's investment return and cash value may vary.
6. Variable universal life insurance. This security has universal and variable properties. It provides flexible premium payments, insurance coverage, and an investing account.
7. Long-term care insurance: Long-term care insurance helps manage health care bills as a person ages. It covers long-term custodial care that Medicare and most conventional health insurance plans do not. This risk-management program helps cover the high cost of long-term elder or custodial care.

Exchanges 1035

The IRS lets individuals substitute a life insurance policy they own for one that covers the same individual without taxing the investment profits accrued in the original policy. It has caveats, which one must know before exchanging (Insurance, n.d.). When considering a 1035 exchange, thoroughly analyze both annuities. Unless one intends to maintain the new annuity for a long time, it may be best to keep the old one to avoid the new surrender fee term. Also, when surrendering an annuity for cash and purchasing a new one, one must pay taxes on the surrender.

Life Settlements

A senior settlement, or life settlement, includes selling a life insurance policy to a third party for more than its cash surrender value but less than its net death benefit.

The National Association of Insurance Commissions (NAIC) provides customer alerts, insurance product information, a glossary, and more.

Variable Annuities

A variable annuity is a contract between the insured and an insurance company that involves monthly payments starting immediately or later. One may buy a variable annuity contract with a single or several installments. It is a long-term investment with complex tax rules. The main advantages are lifelong income payments and death protection (Variable annuity, n.d.).

Investment in mutual funds is typical for variable annuities. However, they vary from mutual funds in key ways:

1. Variable annuities provide lifetime payments to the insured or nominated beneficiary.
2. Variable annuities provide death benefits. If you die before the insurer begins paying, your beneficiary will get a fixed sum, usually at least the purchase payments.
3. Variable annuities defer taxes. The annuity income and investment gains are tax-free until withdrawal. One may move money between investment options in a variable annuity without paying taxes.
4. Upon withdrawing from a variable annuity, earnings are subject to regular income tax rates.

Investment options like IRAs and employer-sponsored 401(k) plans provide tax-deferred growth and other benefits. Investors should max out IRA and 401(k) investments before investing in variable annuities.

Also, investing in a variable annuity via a tax-advantaged retirement plan like 401(k) or IRA does not provide extra tax benefits.

Assumed Interest Rate

Insurance firms compute the first payment using the assumed interest rate. It sets expectations for future payments. Variable annuities provide bigger profits but more risk than fixed annuities. As returns from variable annuities can vary, insurers calculate an assumed interest rate (AIR) for variable annuities, estimating the rise of the annuity. AIR, as a benchmark, can anticipate variable annuity payouts. Bigger AIR means greater payments. Typically, variable annuities have 3%–7% AIRs.

The AIR only applies when the investor receives payments and holds annuity units during the payout period. Unit accumulation during the accumulation stage or postponed benefits do not matter to the assumed interest rate.

Investors get annuity payments depending on their annuity unit count multiplied by the annuity unit value. The investor's payment and unit value are constant when performance equals AIR. Choosing a realistic AIR is crucial. The investor's payout and annuity unit value will decline if the AIR is too high. If the account outperforms the AIR, the annuity unit's value and investor's payout would grow.

Rules Safeguarding Variable Annuity

Variable annuities are a prominent source of investor grievances to FINRA due to their complexities and dubious sales strategies.

1. FINRA rule 2111 (Suitability) amply clarifies which clients and under what conditions are suitable for making specific and general investments under a member's or related person's recommendations.
2. FINRA rule 2330 (Members' Responsibilities Regarding Deferred

Variable Annuities) to improve businesses' accountability and supervisory processes and safeguard investors who buy or sell them.

    a. Principal review: A registered principal must approve a customer's deferred variable annuity application before sending it to the insurance company. After receiving a complete application, a supervisory office must act within seven working days. The registered representative's recommendation determines whether a principal may authorize the transaction.

    b. Firm surveillance: Companies must record and maintain surveillance procedures that fulfill their standards. Firms must track brokers' variable annuity misconduct and take action.

3. FINRA rule 2320 (Variable Contracts of an Insurance Company) has essential cash and non-monetary compensation criteria for variable annuity sales.

Annuitization

Annuitization has existed for centuries, but life insurance firms made it a public contract in the 1800s. Individuals may contract with a life insurance company to exchange a lump sum capital for a guarantee of regular payments for the predetermined period or annuitant's life.

Its key features are:

1. Periodic payments of earnings.
2. Annuities might be for a set time or life.
3. The annuitant or a surviving spouse in a joint life contract may receive annuity payments.
4. Annuitants may arrange for beneficiaries to receive a part of the annuity sum upon death.

The computation considers the annuitant's age, life expectancy, and the insurer's expected interest rate. The ensuing payout rate specifies how much the insurance will pay to repay the annuitant's balance plus interest after the payment period.

Beneficiaries

Beneficiaries obtain benefits from other people's assets. Beneficiaries typically inherit these advantages. Life insurance, retirement accounts, brokerage accounts, bank accounts, and other financial products may select beneficiaries.

Life Option

The life option is an annuity payment system. It pledges lifetime annuity payments. That period is unpredictable; thus, the life option carries financial risk for both the annuitant and the insurance company paying them.

Life expectancy

The investor's lifespan entails the payout duration. If the estimate is 25 years during the contract, the insurance must pay an annuity up to that time and return the principal on term completion. If the annuitant lives longer than expected, the life insurance must continue paying until death. In this annuity insurance, the life insurer takes the risk of a longer lifespan.

Longevity Risk

Longevity risk occurs when life expectancies and survival rates surpass estimates or pricing assumptions, requiring insurance firms or pension funds to provide more cash flow.

Period Certain

Period certain annuities let customers determine when and how long they will receive annuities and which beneficiaries will profit, unlike the more traditional life, lifetime, or pure life annuity, which pays out for life regardless of retirement length.

Period certain annuities provide "income for a guaranteed period." Insurance firms that sell annuities might use several names and descriptions. It's differences from a life annuity are:

Lifelong Annuity	Period certain
A lifelong annuity benefits the annuitant until death. The deceased's estate or beneficiary will not profit after that.	A period certain option ensures that the deceased annuitant's estate or beneficiary may continue receiving annuity payments until the prefixed timeframe within the period certain.
An annuity provides retirement income.	An annuitant can determine the time to start the benefit and its duration to match a period certain option to their retirement and estate planning needs and their life expectancies.
Its duration is for the life of the annuitant.	Standard times for a period certain are 10, 15, or 20 years.

Investment Risks

Returning loaned money to a lender is *repayment*. It usually involves monthly payments toward the principal—the debt—and interest, a charge for the "privilege" of helping to obtain the money through lending. Some loans enable full repayment at any time. However, there may be early repayment costs.

Everyone must repay loans, a financial obligation. Most individuals have vehicle, mortgage, college, or credit card debt. Businesses also handle mortgages, lines of credit, bonds, and other structured corporate debt. Falling behind on payments may lead to involuntary bankruptcy, late fees, and poor credit ratings.

Risk in finance is the likelihood that a situation or investment may not meet expectations or return. Investment risk implies partial or whole loss. Risk quantification considers past conduct and outcomes. Finance risk measurements include standard deviation. Many ideas, measurements, and methodologies exist to assess, evaluate, and manage risks academically, including standard deviation, beta, Value at Risk (VaR), and the Capital Asset Pricing Model (CAPM). Standard deviation compares asset price volatility to historical averages over time. Understanding risk basics and quantification makes sensible investment risk management possible.

Personality, lifestyle, and age are important determinants in individual investment management and risk. Each investor's risk profile defines their risk tolerance. The *time horizon* and *liquidity of investments* are important factors in risk assessment. If investors need cash soon, they are less inclined to engage in high-risk or non-liquid assets and more likely to buy risk-free products.

Time horizons will also affect individual investing portfolios. Younger investors with longer retirement horizons may be ready to take on greater-risk investments with larger rewards. Since older investors require more capital, their risk tolerance is different.

If risks rise, investors expect larger profits to offset it.

A risk-return relationship is a key financial concept. Investors who are willing to take more risk may earn more as a way of compensation. Thus, a US Treasury bond is one of the safest investments and yields less than a business bond. Corporate bonds provide a greater return due to their increased default risk.

Riskless Securities

Riskless securities are investments that have a low risk and estimated return. These securities are popular with all sorts of investors for emergency savings or liquid assets.

Certificates of deposits (CDs), government money market accounts, and US Treasury notes are risk-free investments. Financial modeling traditionally uses the 30-day US Treasury bill as a risk-free security. The US government guarantees it, and its short maturity date reduces interest rate risk.

Savings and CDs are risk-free, but bank failures may cost. FDIC insures up to $250,000 per investor per bank; anything over that risks bank failure. Even riskless US government bonds face risks if the government defaults on its debt. In 2011, Standard & Poor's lowered the government's credit rating due to a debt ceiling impasse. Financial markets shook, slowing economic growth. It happened again in 2023.

Risk Types

Systematic Risks

Systematic risks, sometimes called market risks, may influence the whole economic market or a substantial portion. Market risk is the danger of losing investments due to political and macroeconomic issues impacting market performance. Market risk is difficult to minimize with portfolio diversification. Systematic risks include interest rates, inflation, currency, liquidity, and national and socio-political risks.

Unsystematic Risk

Unsystematic risk is also known as specific risk or idiosyncratic risk. Unsystematic risk is the possibility of losing money due to company- or industry-specific threats. Examples include:

- **A management change.**

  - A product recall.
  - A legislative change affecting sales.
  - A new rival has the potential to capture market share.

Diversifying assets helps investors control unsystematic risk.

Credit Risk

Credit or default risk is when a borrower cannot pay its obligatory loan interest or principal per contract. Bond investors are especially concerned about this danger. Government bonds, particularly federal ones, offer the lowest default risk and returns. Bonds with a reduced default possibility are investor grade.

Corporate bonds have a high default risk and higher interest rates. High-yield or junk bonds have a greater default risk than investment-grade bonds.

Interest Rate Risk

Interest rate risk occurs when an investment's value changes due to changes in the spread between two rates, absolute levels of interest rates, the yield curve, or any other factors connected to the interest rate. This risk impacts bond values more directly than equities and is a significant concern for bondholders—bond prices in the secondary market decline when interest rates increase and vice versa.

Fixed-income assets have a negative correlation between interest rates and security prices. When interest rates rise, the opportunity cost of keeping bonds rises due to the higher expense of forgoing a potentially more profitable investment. As interest rates increase, the attractiveness of bond rates decreases. When interest rates surpass the fixed rate of certain bonds, investors shift to assets that provide greater interest rates. Securities issued before the interest rate change may only remain competitive with fresh issuances by reducing their pricing.

Interest rate risk and reinvestment risk are interconnected. Investors may be unable to reinvest cash flows like interest or dividends at the same rate of return as the initial investment. Reinvestment risk is significant for bonds because of time-dependent variations in interest rates. Laddering, diversifying, and choosing assets with multiple maturity dates helps reduce reinvestment risk.

Purchasing Power Risk

Purchasing power is the monetary value representing the quantity of products or services one may buy with a single unit of currency. It may deteriorate gradually due to inflation. Ascending prices lead to a drop in purchasing power. Purchasing power is synonymous with a currency's buying power. Buying power in investing refers to the credit amount accessible to an investor determined by the current marginable securities in the customer's brokerage account. Marginable securities are stocks, futures, bonds, etc., that one can trade on a margin. Margin trading concerns borrowing dollars from a broker to purchase assets. Brokers restrict the securities available to minimize the risk of financial loss. The Federal Reserve determines which assets may be collateral for margin trading, and brokers provide a list of marginable securities to their customers within that category.

Call Risk

Call risk is the financial impact on bondholders when a bond issuer decides to redeem or "call" their existing bonds before the maturity date. Callable bonds often have a set call price and call date, enabling the issuer to buy back the bonds at their discretion.

Fixed-income securities investors encounter call risk while investing in callable bonds, which might result in diminished profits if the issuer decides to redeem the bonds before the anticipated maturity date. Investing in callable bonds might introduce unpredictability of call risk.

Causes of Call Risk

1. Falling Interest Rates: When interest rates fall, issuers can refinance their debt at a lower cost. They have to call their existing bonds and issue new bonds at lower rates. It is unfavorable for bondholders. They may have to reinvest the proceeds from the called bonds below par interest rates. It reduces overall returns.
2. Financial Condition of the Issuer: If a bond issuer's financial condition betters, they may opt to call their existing bonds. It will reduce their interest payments or remodel their debt. This decision can poorly affect bondholders. They lose interest payments and may have to reinvest the proceeds at lower rates. It can also take time to find similar investment opportunities.
3. Market Conditions: Transformations in market conditions, such as more demand for the issuer's products or services, can strengthen the issuer's financial position, raising the possibility that they will call their bonds. Consequently, redeeming the bonds earlier exposes investors to call risk.
4. Regulatory Modifications: Regulatory changes can also induce an issuer to call their bonds. For instance, tax law or industry regulation changes

may enable issuers to call their bonds to benefit from further financing options or, sometimes, agree with revised provisions.

Types of Callable Securities

Different types of callable securities are callable bonds and preferred stocks.

Callable Bonds

Callable bonds are a type of debt securities. They give the issuer the right to redeem the bonds before the maturity dates. Some types of callable bonds include the following:

1. Municipal Bonds: State and local governments issue these bonds to fund public projects. The callable nature of these bonds allows the issuer to redeem them before maturity to refinance their debts or modify their borrowing expenses.
2. Corporate Bonds: Some corporate bonds are callable, letting the issuer redeem them before maturity.
3. Mortgage-Backed Securities: Mortgage-backed securities (MBS) may be callable, permitting the issuer to redeem them before maturity if mortgage prepayment rates rise or the issuer desires to recreate their portfolio.

Preferred Stocks

Preferred stocks designate an ownership stake in a company to the investors. They typically furnish a fixed dividend payment. Some are callable and include the following:

1. Callable preferred stocks: These grant the issuing business the right to redeem the shares at a prefixed price before maturity.
2. Convertible preferred stocks: Investors can convert these types of preferred stock into a prefixed number of common shares at the shareholder's preference. They can be callable, and the issuer can redeem them before

their conversion date. It will limit dilution or help manage their capital structure.

Measuring Call Risks

Investors can evaluate call risk by weighing several factors, such as yield to worst (YTW), yield to call (YTC), bond duration and convexity, and call price and call date.

1. YTC: A callable bond's yield to call calculates its potential return for redeeming it on its call date. YTC may assist investors in choosing a callable bond by comparing its return to similar-risk bonds.
2. YTW: Given all call and maturity opportunities, YTW is the lowest bond yield an investor may earn. YTW calculates the minimal callable bond return, including call risk.
3. Call price and call date: The call price is the issuer's specified redeeming price, while the call date is the bond's earliest call date. To assess call risk, investors should consider the call price and date.
4. Duration and convexity: assesses a bond's relationship to interest rate fluctuations, whereas convexity indicates its duration's changes with the fluctuation of interest rates. By studying its duration and convexity, investors may better appreciate how call risk may impact a bond's price and yield in various interest rate conditions.

How to Manage Call Rates

1. Diversification, using bond funds and ETFs, laddering bond portfolios, and surveillance of interest rates may help investors lessen call risk.
2. Diversification: Diversifying bond portfolios with non-callable or callable bonds with different call dates reduces call risk. This method reduces call risk on fixed-income assets.
3. Laddering bonds portfolios: Laddering spreads reinvestment risk by investing in bonds with different maturities. Avoiding simultaneous calls on all portfolio bonds reduces call risk.
4. Bond funds and ETFs: Using bonds and ETFs may reduce call risk by offering exposure to a diverse portfolio of bonds and offsetting the effects of early redemptions.

5. Tracking interest rates: Investors may anticipate call risk by monitoring interest rate changes. Investors may modify their bond portfolio to reduce bond calls if interest rates fall.

6. Call provisions and protection procedures may reduce call risk for investors and include the following:

   a. Call protection periods: Specific and prefixed call protection periods prevent the issuer from prematurely calling the bond. Investors may use this to predict the bond's revenue stream and reduce call risk.

   b. Make-whole call conditions: In case of an early call, make-whole call clauses oblige the issuer to pay bondholders a premium based on future coupon payments.

   c. Soft-call clauses: These safeguard investors by ensuring the issuer calls the bond only under certain situations, such as a credit rating change or a major financial event affecting the issuer adversely.

   d. Step-up callable bonds: This feature rises in coupon rates with call dates. This structure encourages the issuer to call the bond when the coupon rate increases, giving investors higher payouts if not called promptly.

Significance of Call Risk for the Investors

1. Reinvestment risk: Investors face reinvestment risk when they have to reinvest funds from called bonds at a lower interest rate. It can hurt an investor's fixed-income portfolio.

2. Price risk: A callable bond's market value may fall owing to interest rate fluctuations or call probability. If interest rates fall, the bond's price may rise, increasing the risk of it being called and causing losses in capital for investors who have to dispose of it before it is called.

3. Income risk: When a bond issuer calls, investors lose income predictability, particularly when called at the wrong moment or if the investor cannot locate a substitute investment

4. Credit risk: Bond issuers can default on interest or principal payments, creating credit risk. It is not directly linked to call risk. Even then, it can influence bond calls since issuers with better credit ratings may call their bonds to refinance at cheaper interest rates (Tamplin, 2023).

Liquidity Risk

A business may struggle to meet its short-term financial commitments if it cannot convert assets into money without incurring significant losses. Financial organizations and companies are vulnerable to this risk, which affects their operations and stability.

Two basic features of liquidity risk are market and financing liquidity risks. Insufficient market coverage or disturbances may prevent a company from undertaking transactions at market pricing, causing *market liquidity risk*. The inability to secure enough funds to satisfy financial commitments is *funding liquidity risk*.

Liquidity risk is a *generalized feature across financial sectors* and can affect banks, commercial and industrial enterprises, and even some individual investors. Following precautions ensure the minimization of liquidity risks to prevent business interruptions, financial losses, brand harm, and insolvency or bankruptcy in severe instances that may, by extension, harm the nation's economy.

1. *Regulatory frameworks like Basel that sets strict liquidity standards* require banks and financial institutions to control liquidity risk to safeguard financial stability and depositor interests. Corporations must manage liquidity risk to satisfy operational and financial obligations with enough cash or credit lines.
2. Businesses must *diversify capital* and *predict cash flow*.
3. Managing liquidity risk assures businesses have *adequate cash* or *liquid assets* for short-term requirements and commitments without undergoing huge losses.

Insolvency

1. Insolvency occurs when a person or company cannot pay their debts---reflecting financial distress.
2. In insolvency, liabilities exceed the firm's worth. Liabilities also occur when a debtor cannot pay.
3. Several situations can hamper cash flow, which may spur insolvency.

4. Insolvency procedures may include legal action against the insolvent party and asset liquidation to pay off obligations.
5. Insolvent businesses and individuals may approach creditors directly to renegotiate debts and pay in affordable installments. It is known as restructuring of debts. For honest restructuring, the business owner must create a realistic strategy to cut costs and keep operations going.
6. Creditors are usually willing to follow this delayed repayment approach to prevent further damages.

Bankruptcy

1. Bankruptcy releases individuals and businesses from debt obligations.
2. Bankruptcy grants creditors repayment opportunities.
3. The US Bankruptcy Code governs bankruptcy in federal courts.

   a. Chapter 7 bankruptcy: Most individuals apply for Chapter 7 bankruptcy, eliminating unsecured obligations like credit cards and medical expenses. Chapter 7 bankruptcy involves selling assets like family heirlooms, second houses, or investments like stocks or bonds to pay off debt. People with no valuable assets and only exempt property such as household items, clothes, trade equipment, and a personal car up to a specified value may be unable to return their unsecured loan.

      i. Chapter 13 bankruptcy: Those who make excessive money for filing Chapter 7 bankruptcy might apply under Chapter 13, a wage earner's plan. It helps people and organizations with stable incomes construct debt payback programs, which may include three- to five-year payments. The courts let these debtors retain all their property, even the nonexempt ones, to repay their creditors.

   b. Chapter 11 bankruptcy: Businesses apply for Chapter 11 bankruptcy to reorganize and survive in business. Chapter 11 bankruptcy allows corporations to plan for profits, minimize expenses, and grow income. Preferred shareholders may get compensation, but common stockholders will come in last. In rare circumstances, individuals may also declare Chapter 11 bankruptcy.

4. Bankruptcy stays on credit records for years, making future borrowing harder.
5. An individual or corporation may start over by legally waiving unpayable debts in bankruptcy. Creditors may recover some of the individual's or business's dissolved assets. Bankruptcy gives consumers and businesses another credit opportunity, which helps the economy. It may also help creditors recover some debt.

A *bankruptcy court* decides for debtors whether to file and whether to dismiss their debts. The United States Trustee Program of the Department of Justice appoints trustees to represent debtor estates in bankruptcy proceedings. The debtor and judge seldom interact until a creditor objects. Bankruptcy procedures relieve debtors of their responsibilities by issuing a discharge order.

With a legal discharge order, a debtor is no longer compelled to pay the debts listed in the order. After the discharge order is in effect, creditors mentioned on it cannot lawfully collect from the debtor.

However, not all debts are dischargeable. Some examples are tax claims, unlisted debts, child support or alimony payments, personal injury debts, and government debts. Secured creditors may enforce a valid lien against the debtor's property.

Debtors may not have discharge rights. Courts notify creditors about bankruptcy petitions, which they might oppose by filing a complaint before the deadline. It leads to an adversarial process to collect debt or enforce a lien.

Forbearance, Loan Modification, and Offer in Compromise

These are alternatives to bankruptcy. *Forbearance* lets debtors stop paying for a specific time, and repayment plans stretch to lower monthly payments.

A *loan modification* permanently lowers the interest rates and simplifies repayment.

An *offer in compromise* may enable one to settle with the IRS for less than one owes. The IRS often provides monthly payment arrangements for taxpayers who can't pay their taxes simultaneously.

Some Financial Health Measuring Tools

Capital Asset Pricing Model (CAPM)

The CAPM model links systematic or investment risks to asset returns, notably for equities. A linear connection exists between risk and investment return in this finance model. The concept is based on an asset's beta, which is the risk-free rate, usually the Treasury bill rate, and the equity risk premium, or market return minus the risk-free rate. CAPM evaluates systematic risk. Finance uses it to price risky securities and forecast asset returns for asset risk and capital cost (Kenton, 2023).

Formula

$$ER_i = R_f + \beta_i (ER_m - R_f)$$

ER_i = expected return of investment

R_f = Risk-free rate

B_i = Investment's beta

$(ER_m - R_f)$ = Market risk Premium

CAPM Uses

1. Calculating a stock's risk
2. Time value of money
3. Predicted return
4. The fair value of a stock or whether a stock's price matches its expected return

Bankruptcy Risk Measurements

Bond Ratio

The bond ratio measures a bond issuer's leverage by evaluating bond values and due dates. Financial instruments like bonds and other debt are examples of leverage as borrowed capital.

Formula

Bond ratio = (bond values due after one year)/(bond values due after one year plus equity capital)

Debt-to-equity (D/E) Ratio

The D/E ratio, a gearing ratio, measures a company's financial leverage by dividing its total liabilities by its shareholder equity. The D/E ratio is crucial in corporate finance. It measures how much a corporation relies on debt rather than its funds.

Formula

D/E ratio = Total liabilities / Total shareholder's equity

Liquidity Measurements

Net Working Capital (NWC)

The NWC is the gap between a company's current assets (cash, accounts receivable/unpaid bills, inventories, and completed goods) and present liabilities (accounts payable and loans). It is a typical indicator of an organization's short-term health.

Formula

Working capital = Existing assets - Present liabilities

Current Ratio

The current or working capital ratio assesses a company's capacity to pay short-term or one-year commitments. It advises investors and analysts on how a firm may optimize its current assets balance sheet to pay its present debt and other payables.

A current ratio at the industry average or slightly above is acceptable. A lower current ratio than the industry norm may imply distress or default. If a company's current ratio is high relative to its peers, management may not employ assets effectively.

Formula

Current ratio = Present assets / Present liabilities

Acid-Test Ratio

A company's most liquid assets are quick assets. They are its accounts receivable, marketable securities, and cash or equivalents. Companies employ quick assets to create financial ratios, especially the quick ratio, for decision-making.

The acid-test ratio, the quick ratio, examines balance sheet data to determine whether a company can pay its short-term obligations. A ratio of 1.0 or above implies a corporation can pay its short-term commitments, while less than 1.0 indicates it may struggle.

Formula

Quick ratio = CA – Inventory – PE / Present liabilities

CA = Current assets

PE = Prepaid expenditures

Quick ratio = C&E + MS +AR / Present liabilities

C&E = Cash and equivalents

MS = Marketable securities

AR = Accounts receivable

Inventory Turnover

Inventory turnover measures a company's inventory turnover compared to its cost of goods sold (COGS). To compute the average number of days it takes to sell inventory, a corporation divides the duration, usually a fiscal year, by the inventory turnover ratio.

The inventory turnover ratio may improve pricing, production, marketing, and buying choices. This efficiency ratio measures how well a corporation utilizes its assets.

Formula

Inventory turnover = COGS / Average value of inventory

COGS = Cost of goods sold

Cash Flow

Company cash flow is net cash and cash equivalents flowing in and out of a business. Inflows are money received, and outflows are expenditures. Positive cash flows and long-term free cash flow (FCF) increase shareholder value. The minus is FCF.

FC F = Cash from regular company operations – CapEx

CapEx = Money for capital expenditures

Profitability

Profit margin is a company's return on goods or services after direct and indirect expenses. It is written as a percentage.

Formula

Net profit margin = (Net profit / Total revenue for the year) × 100

Gross profit margin = (Gross profit / Total revenue for the year) × 100

Net Asset Value (NAV)

Company NAV is near to or equivalent to its book value. High-growth firms cost more than their NAV. Compare the NAV to the market capitalization (MC) to find an undervalued or overvalued stock. Several financial evaluations employ NAV or enterprise value.

Formula

NAV = (Assets – Liabilities) / Total shares

Book Value Per Share (BVPS)

BVPS is a simple calculation that estimates a company's per-share worth based on the amount of common shareholders' equity in the business.

Formula

BVPS = Shareholders' equity / Outstanding common shares

Interest Coverage Ratio

The Interest coverage ratio reveals how efficiently a business can pay interest on its outstanding debts. The interest coverage ratio is also known as the times interest earned (TIE) ratio. Loaners, investors, and creditors use this method to assess a company's risk compared to present or future borrowing tendencies.

Formula

Interest coverage ratio = EBIT/Time

EBIT = Earnings before interest and taxes

EPS

Price-to-Earnings Ratio (P/E)

Most investors and analysts evaluate stocks using the P/E. A good P/E for one industry may be low for another, so comparing corresponding firms is useful.

Investors use the P/E ratio to compare a stock's market value to its earnings. Based on previous or projected profits, it reflects what the market will pay for a stock.

Formula

P/E ratio = Present price / most current earnings per share

Dividend Payment Ratio (DPR)

A company's dividend payment ratio evaluates its targets. However, company maturity is crucial for analyzing DPR.

Formula

DPR = Dividends disbursed / Net proceeds

Or,

DPR = DPS / EPS

DPS = Dividend per share

EPS = Earnings per share

EPS

EPS quantifies a company's profits per share. Basic EPS does not account for convertible securities' dilutive repercussions.

Dilution occurs when share numbers grow, such as via a fresh issuance. Issued shares to investors increase the number of shares outstanding and lower EPS. It may lower stock prices.

Formula

EPS = (Net income-preferred dividends) / weighted average number of common shares outstanding

Diluted EPS = (Net income-preferred stock dividends) / (Average outstanding shares+dilutive shares)

Current Yield

The current yield of a discount bond exceeds the yearly coupon rate due to the inverse relationship between the bond yield and market price. Premium bonds yield less than their yearly coupon rate, whereas par bonds yield the same. The current yield varies from the yearly coupon rate due to changes in interest rate market dynamics, depending on investor inflation forecasts. Current yield and additional indicators like YTM, Yield to the first call, etc., help investors make educated investment decisions.

Formula

Current yield of bond = Yearly coupon payment / Present market price

Competitiveness

Return on Equity (ROE)

ROE measures financial performance. Shareholder equity is a company's assets less its debt; hence, ROE is the return on net assets.

ROE measures a company's profitability and efficiency. A company's management generates revenue and growth from equity financing more efficiently with a higher ROE.

Formula

ROE = Net income / Shareholders' equity. You must use Microsoft Excel sheet to calculate ROE.

Calculating it by DuPont's formula:

1. ROE = NPM × Asset turnover × Equity multiplier; where NPM = Net profit margin
2. ROE = (EBT/S) × (S/A) × (A/E) × (1–TR); where EBT = Earning before tax, S=Sales, A =Assets, E = Equity, and TR = Tax rates

Instead of focusing on one ratio, the three- and five-step equations examine what is happening in an organization to understand its ROE better. Always compare financial statement ratios to the company's and competitor's records.

Chapter Four: Retirement Planning and Taxation

Retirement plans and taxation are perhaps the most crucial aspects of an investor's future planning. Every responsible individual aims to earn enough to provide for their present needs and also to secure the future when they retire from work and will be living on pension schemes.

Employer-Sponsored Plans and ERISA

Various labor and tax laws govern employee pension programs. ERISA's Title I provisions addressed public concerns about mishandling and exploiting private pension plan money.

In 1963, Studebaker shuttered its Indiana manufacturing, affecting almost 4,000 pension plan beneficiaries with underfunded schemes. In the 1960s and 70s, the Teamsters' Central States Pension Fund raised awareness of retirement account fiduciary misconduct. The fund made dubious loans to Las Vegas casinos and real estate projects.

These are two instances of the anomalies ERISA first sought to rectify. The US House of Representatives enacted the measure in February 1974, and the Senate approved it the following month. President Gerald Ford signed ERISA on Sept. 2, 1974.

Key Features

1. The federal statute ERISA regulates employer-sponsored retirement plans and plan fiduciaries. The law determines how long a person must work before joining a plan, earning benefits, and having a non-forfeitable entitlement to them. It sets precise financial standards that require retirement plan sponsors to finance the plan adequately.
2. The 1974 statute has undergone many modifications. For instance, lawmakers lowered employers' age restrictions for retirement plan participation and extended workers' leave time before losing their plan's vesting term. ERISA modifications also happened due to healthcare legislation. For instance, the 1985 COBRA program guaranteed health insurance coverage following work changes.
3. ERISA bans fiduciaries from misuse of money and specifies minimum retirement plan enrollment, vesting, benefit accrual, and financing criteria.
4. Retirement plan members may sue for benefits and fiduciary responsibility violations.
5. The ERISA protects retirement savings against creditors, bankruptcy, and civil litigation. If a business goes bankrupt, retirement savings remain secure, and creditors cannot claim on them.

ERISA-Covered Plans

ERISA-covered plans include:

1. Employer-sponsored retirement plans

    A. 401(k)s
    B. Pensions
    C. Deferred compensation plans
    D. Profit-sharing plans.

2. Non-retirement plans

    A. Health maintenance organizations accounts HMOs
    B. Flexible spending accounts FSAs
    C. Disability insurance

D. Life insurance.

Plan Fiduciaries

ERISA protects the plan's assets by requiring fiduciary responsibilities for those who exercise discretionary power or control over the management of plans or assets, plan administration, or investment advice for compensation. Trustees, administrators, and investment committee members are plan fiduciaries.

Making an investment policy statement (IPS) is the obligation of the *investment committee*. The IPS must have:

1. Clear due diligence methods to choose and supervise investment options
2. Plan performance benchmarks
3. Criteria for choosing and assessing investment managers and replacing them
4. Annual review to identify plan management discrepancies

Committee members have the following obligations:

1. Compare plan performance against IPS benchmarks
2. Check any changes in the investment management team, investing strategy, fees or charges, and assets under management (AUM) to ensure they meet the plan's investment objectives and parameters.
3. Keep meticulous records of meeting proceedings and outcomes. All investment documents should be in the committee's fiduciary audit file (Kagan, 2022).

Fiduciaries must manage the plan exclusively for members and beneficiaries, delivering benefits and paying plan expenditures. Fiduciaries must behave responsibly and diversify the plan's assets to avoid excessive losses. Furthermore, they must follow plan provisions that comply with ERISA. They must prevent conflicts of interest. They may not act on behalf of the plan to benefit other fiduciaries, service providers, or the plan sponsor.

Fiduciaries who violate these rules may be personally responsible for restoring plan losses or gains from unlawful plan asset usage. For fiduciaries who violate their obligations, courts may remove them.

Small Businesses and ERISA

Many ERISA requirements are complicated. It can dissuade some small company owners from setting up employee retirement accounts. These firms may avoid certain complicated laws using alternatives. Small firms with 100 or less workers may utilize SIMPLE IRAs. Unlike qualified retirement plans like 401(k)s, ERISA-covered tax-deferred retirement savings programs don't need reporting or administration. The Setup is also more straightforward for SIMPLE IRAs.

Employers must follow ERISA standards on eligibility and how the business manages employee contributions. They must adequately describe the plan's elements in a brief plan description.

ERISA and Healthcare

ERISA protects workers participating in various healthcare plans with the following attributes. The legislation excludes plans without these requirements.

1. Mandatory plans
2. Plans that obtain employer contributions
3. Plans that delineate modes of fund management

Under the law, providers must disclose all plan facts to participants, including the following:

1. Eligibility of coverage
2. Medical, accident, unemployment, and other employee benefits
3. Full disclosure of rates, deductibles, and copays
4. Networks and claim-making methods
5. The Affordable Care Act (ACA) modified the statute. It required firms with 50 or more employees to provide healthcare, set a cap on out-of-pocket

costs, and stop denial of coverage due to preexisting conditions, which altered the statute.

Some individuals may remain eligible under their parent's plan until 26 years of age.

ERISA's Administration

Employee Benefits Security Administration (EBSA) under the DOL regulates ERISA. This organization educates and helps workers, businesses, and plan administrators about retirement and healthcare programs.

Plan participants must receive updates and statements in compliance with ERISA. Plan administrators must send members first-quarter statements in the second quarter, second-quarter statements in the third quarter, and so forth. Participants must get appropriate notifications and paperwork. Plans must also follow plan document provisions, offer 12-month fee disclosures, timely notify members of plan modifications, and maintain deposits and deferrals on schedule. Plan administrators may handle the paperwork themselves. They may also outsource. However, this doesn't exonerate the administrator of its fiduciary duty to participants.

Retirement Plans

The Employee Retirement Income Security or ERISA regulates two varieties of retirement plans. They are defined benefit and defined contribution retirement plans.

ERISA provides minimal rules for most voluntarily created private business retirement and health plans to safeguard plan members. ERISA requires retirement plans to equip participants with plan information, including essential plan elements and funding; sets minimum requirements for participation, vesting, benefit accrual, and funding; confers fiduciary duties on those who control and manage plan assets; establishes a grievance and appeals process for plan beneficiaries; and allows participants to file for benefits and fiduciary infringements. It guarantees some reimbursements via the Pension Benefit Guaranty Corporation if a defined benefit plan is discontinued.

ERISA applies to:

1. Anyone who works for a partnership
2. Limited liability company
3. S-corporation
4. C-corporation
5. Nonprofit organization
6. Businesses even when there is only one employee.

ERISA generally does not apply to government, religious, or employee plans that are primarily for worker's compensation, unemployment, or disability compliance. ERISA does not cover unfunded excess benefit plans or programs principally for nonresident aliens outside the US.

Defined Benefit Plan

A defined benefit plan guarantees a defined amount of retirement monthly payout. The plan may specify the payout in dollars, such as $200 per month upon retirement. It may also calculate a benefit using a plan formula that takes into account income and service, such as 2% of the average salary for the past 5 years of work for every year of service. Within certain limits, the Pension Benefit Guaranty Corporation (PBGC) of the Federal government insurance protects most standard defined benefit plans.

Defined Contribution Plan

A defined contribution plan does not guarantee specific amounts of retirement benefits. The employee or employer, or both, can contribute to the employee's plan account, often at a specified amount like 3% of earnings yearly. The employee invests these contributions through the corporations. The employee receives the account balance after contributions and investment profits or losses. The account's value fluctuates with investment values. Some examples of defined contribution plans are profit-sharing plans, employee stock ownership, 401(k), and 403(b).

Simplified Employee Pension Plan (SEP)

An SEP refers to a simple retirement savings plan. SEPs enable employees to make tax-favored contributions to their individual retirement accounts (IRAs). SEPs have limited reporting and disclosure obligations. SEP employees must open an IRA to receive company contributions. Employers may not create Salary Reduction SEPs anymore. However, employers may create Savings Incentive Match Plan for Employees (SIMPLE) IRA programs along with salary reduction contributions. A SIMPLE IRA plan lets companies and workers contribute to traditional IRAs for workers. It is appropriate for small firms without retirement plans as a start-up savings strategy. For an employer with a salary reduction SEP, it may be possible for them to continue accepting salary reduction contributions.

Profit Sharing Plan

A profit sharing plan, also known as a stock bonus plan, is a variety of defined contribution plans where the plan itself or the employer determines the yearly contribution amount. The plan organizes yearly contributions among participants using a formula. A profit sharing or stock bonus plan may incorporate a 401(k).

A 401(k) Plan

A 401(k) plan refers to a defined contribution plan, either cash or deferred. Employees may choose to have some of their pay donated to the 401(k) plan before taxes. They defer obtaining this amount of salary from the employer. Employers may match these donations. Employees may only defer a certain amount yearly. An employer must inform employees of any limitations. Participants in 401(k) plans contribute part of their pay and often control their investments to fund their retirement.

Employee Stock Ownership Plan (ESOP)

An ESOP is a defined contribution plan that invests mostly in employer stocks. Companies often employ ESOPs for succession planning, enabling owners to sell their shares and transfer out of the firm flexibly. The firm creates an ESOP trust.

1. The corporation may contribute funds to acquire stock from current owners at fair market value or release new shares if the owner does not wish to sell.
2. If the firm lacks initial funds, the ESOP might borrow to acquire shares while the corporation provides funds to repay the debt.
3. Employee shares in the trust are often based on their salaries. Employees who stay longer for the firm get increasing share rights, known as vesting. Typically, full-time workers over 21 are eligible for the plan. Employee ownership rights include control and voting rights inside the firm.
4. When employees quit, the corporation must purchase their stock at fair market value unless a public market for the shares exists. The employee gets the value of their shares from the trust, often in cash.

Cash Balance Plan

A type of defined benefit is the Cash Balance Plan, which specifies the benefit in terms that are similar to a defined contribution plan. A cash balance plan depicts the promised benefit by account balance. A typical cash balance plan credits a participant's account with a "pay credit" (such as 5% of employer remuneration) and an "interest credit" (fixed or variable) tied to an index like the one-year treasury bill rate each year. Growth and decline in the plan's investment values do not influence the participant's benefits. The employer bears all plan asset investment risks and profits. An account balance represents a participant's cash balance plan benefits. The Pension Benefit Guaranty Corporation (PBGC) ensures the most cash balance and defined benefit plans, with certain exceptions.

The Time Factor

Many firms match employees' 401(k) contributions up to a specific percentage of pay, which may help ensure retirement. By contributing over the limit, one can maximize the reward. One may lose free money if contributing less than the company matches. A retirement nest account may grow significantly with an employer match.

Let's say a 22-year-old earns $40,000, and puts 3% ($1,200) into their 401(k). If this individual continues to earn the same income and make the same contribution each year until 65, they will have $51,600 in their 401(k) after 43 years. Suppose this individual's company matches their 401(k) contributions up to 3% of salary dollar-for-dollar. Employers often match funds, doubling them from $51,600 to $103,200. It means a free $51,600 in the individual's 401(k) account. Any additional investment gain will boost the value of the plan.

Suppose this individual waits a few years before contributing to their 401(k). At 30, they start putting 3% of their $40,000 income into their 401(k). If they retire at 65 with the same income and contribution each year, they will save $82,000 with their contribution and employer's match. Starting at 22 would have saved them roughly 20% more. The sooner one starts saving in retirement plans, the longer one's money can grow, and compound interest may make that growth enormous.

Tax Reduction

In addition to assisting plans for the future, 401(k) contributions provide tax benefits now. Pre-tax earnings go into a standard 401(k) retirement plan. Every dollar saved in this account with pre-tax contributions reduces the current taxable income by the same amount, lowering the annual income tax bill. According to the example above, contributing $1,200 to a typical 401(k) reduces your total taxable income from $40,000 to $38,800. Employer matches 401(k) contributions, and account profits (interest, dividends, and capital gains) are tax-deferred. That means one pays income tax on these savings once removed, usually after retirement.

Qualified Tution Program or a 529 Plan

A state-established and maintained qualified tuition program (QTP), also known as a section 529 plan, allows contributors to prepay or add to an account for a beneficiary's authorized higher education expenses at an approved educational institution. Eligible educational institutions may also create and operate QTPs to prepay beneficiaries' eligible higher education fees. Qualified higher education expenses include those required for the designated beneficiary to gain admission or attend any university, vocational school, college, or other postsecondary educational institution eligible for Department of Education student aid. Approved higher education expenses amounting to $10,000 per year from all of the designated beneficiary's QTPs. It includes:

- Tuition at a religious school.
- An elementary, secondary public.
- Private school from kindergarten to grade 12.

They also cover tuition, books, materials, and equipment for a Secretary of Labor-certified apprenticeship program and qualified education loan repayments in set amounts.

QTP contributions for beneficiaries are limited to their eligible higher education expenditures. The trustee or administrator must inform about the program's donation limit. QTP contributions are not tax-deductible.

The advantages of QTP are:

1. Earnings can accumulate tax-free as long as they are in the account.
2. The beneficiary doesn't typically have to show the earnings from a QTP as income.
3. Distributions are not taxable to pay for qualified higher education expenses. However, if the distribution amount is more than the beneficiary's qualified higher education expenditures, some of the earnings are taxable.
4. One can withdraw amounts to pay principal or interest on a designated beneficiary's or their sibling's student loan. Any individual's distributions for loan repayments are limited to a $10,000 lifetime. Interest paid with these funds doesn't qualify for the deduction of student loan interest.

Features of a 529 Prepaid Tuition Plan for College and Universities

1. Parents, grandparents, and others may prepay at today's tuition rates at qualifying public and private colleges and universities to control future tuition expenditures. Most states ensure that prepaid plan money will match tuition.
2. Prepaid tuition plans have the following features:

    a. It lets one pay for years, credits, or units in one flat sum or installments.
    b. Prepaid tuition plans may cover one to five years of tuition for a two-year community college, a four-year degree program, or a combination of the two.
    c. Some programs include graduate school charges with the contract.
    d. Most state prepaid tuition programs require one or one's children to live in the state to apply, unlike 529 savings plans. Others restrict membership to a set time each year.

3. The plan transfers college tuition directly to the institution when the student is ready to join. If children do not wish to join a college covered by the prepaid tuition plan, all prepaid tuition plans will let them utilize plan money at different educational institutions. Most prepaid plans enable one to transfer the plan to a child's sibling, although age limitations may apply.
4. Unfortunately, most programs would only refund the initial contribution and reduce or eliminate any earned interest if the student or their siblings don't go to college and utilize the plan, or one cancels the prepaid plan for some reason. Some plans include cancellation fees.
5. If an eligible educational institution refunds a distribution from a 529 plan, one can recontribute it to a 529 plan. The contribution is limited to 60 days following the return. These contributions cannot exceed refunds.

A 529 Savings Plan

Teachers, parents, grandparents, and friends can save for qualified college expenses like tuition, fees, room, board, textbooks, computers (if required), and apprenticeship program textbooks, fees, and equipment with 529 savings plans. Guidelines for using these plans to pay for K-12 tuition differ by state and plan.

Before using a 529 savings plan for K-12 tuition, consider that the time period will be shorter than those who save only for college, and withdrawals may not be tax-free in one's state. However, everyone is eligible for federally tax-free qualified withdrawals. It may affect one's financial choices and risk tolerance. Beginning in 2024, beneficiaries of 529 savings plans with at least 15 years of unused money may roll over up to $35,000 into a Roth IRA without penalty or tax obligation, subject to Roth IRA contribution limitations.

A 529 plan lets one invest money on behalf of a beneficiary, usually one's child, although any US citizen or permanent alien with a Social Security number or federal tax identification number may be the beneficiary. Most plans have maximum and minimum contribution restrictions, which vary by state. Since the IRS restricts 529 plan contributions to the beneficiary's eligible higher education costs, money in the 529 savings account may go toward siblings', parents', or grandparents' loans.

Investors may start another 529 plan for the same beneficiary in another state. If one wants one's child to attend an expensive college or graduate school, one can create several 529 plans to enhance one's contributions.

The Municipal Securities Rulemaking Board regulates 529 plans, which are "municipal fund securities" like ABLE accounts. Most colleges and universities, including graduate schools and some international institutions, accept qualified withdrawals from 529 savings plans. Many states provide at least one 529 savings plan with no residency obligations. Thus, one may reside in Portland, contribute to a New York plan, and send their child to California college. However, if the state gives tax benefits to local plan participants, one will lose out if one chooses a 529 plan from another state.

The 529 savings schemes include risks and limits. IRS guidelines limit investment mix changes to two annually. The 529 savings programs do not lock in tuition costs or have the state's guarantee for investment, like prepaid tuition plans. Most 529 savings plan investments are at risk of losing value or not growing enough to cover expenses for college.

Qualified Withdrawals for College Education: Inclusions and Exclusions

1. Only course-required textbooks are within qualified education expenses. Keep receipts and make sure purchases are eligible costs.

2. Using computers and associated equipment and services principally during any year of enrollment at a qualifying educational institution is a qualified cost.

3. Although some prepaid tuition plans provide room and board, most do not. For room and board to be included, the student must have been enrolled for half the time or more. It also does not qualify for paying the actual charge if the student lives in school-run housing.

4. The plan excludes sports, games, and hobby software unless it is primarily instructional.

5. Non qualifying expenses also include amusement or entertainment equipment. Other sources will have to finance insurance, sports, health clubs, and travel and transportation fees. Any portion of the payout made up of profits on contributions will be taxed as regular income and subject to a 10% federal penalty if one withdraws money for nonqualified expenses. Extenuating circumstances may waive the penalty, such as the beneficiary's infirmity or death, a scholarship, or US military school enrollment.

6. Scholarships are exempt from the 10% penalty. A nonqualified withdrawal from the account up to the scholarship amount will incur taxes but not the 10% penalty on a nonqualified withdrawal. Request a scholarship receipt for tax purposes.

7. The administrator of one's 529 savings plan will usually send an annual statement that shows the contributions, earnings, and withdrawals. The student must report appropriately to the IRS, not the program provider. If the withdrawals are less than the qualified higher education expenses (QHEEs), the withdrawals and earnings are tax-free. Taxes and penalties may apply to withdrawals over one's QHEE. People can keep monitoring it since significant college expenses consume much of their 529 funds.

Withdrawing Funds

Some families pay the school straight from their 529 accounts for easier record-keeping and matching payouts to school costs. Ensure the school payment dates and how long it takes to transfer money from the 529 account to the school. Investments sold out of a 529 account and sent to the school may take several days, and the school may take a week to receive the money.

One may also transfer funds from the 529 to one's bank or brokerage account. Many universities prefer bank or brokerage account payments via their website. It is advantageous to make the payments first and then repay oneself from the 529 account or utilize 529 funds to pay expenses from one's bank or brokerage account. However, One must seek the cash during the same calendar year and not the academic year for making payments. A nonqualified withdrawal might result in tax if the timing is wrong.

Another withdrawal option is to distribute money from 529 accounts to a child's account. Using money for nonqualified costs like purchasing a vehicle will show as reportable earnings that can go on the child's tax returns at a lower tax bracket. However, the "kiddie tax" may require some children as old as 23 to pay the tax on unearned earnings at their parents' marginal tax rate. Ask your tax expert whether this applies.

Broker-Sold 529 Programs

Some brokerages and consultants offer some 529 programs. Broker-sold 529 savings may or may not provide state tax benefits and may be more or less costly than state-sold programs. If an investor is comfortable picking a plan and investing alternatives themselves, direct-sold plans may save them money. Brokers must provide clients with 529 plan's disclosure paperwork, which can be on the MSRB's EMMA website.

Conflict with Other Tax Incentives

A 529 plan cannot cover certain educational expenditures for which the federal government gives tax advantages. One should consider whether to claim this tax credit when selecting how much to remove from the 529 account since the IRS will consider it double dipping.

Tax Credits reduce tax obligations, unlike deductions. Investors may claim only one credit each year.

1. The American Opportunity Tax Credit permits undergraduates to deduct the first $2,000 in eligible education costs and 25% of the additional $2,000. In 2024, single parents must have a modified adjusted gross income lower than $90,000 or $180,000 if married and filing jointly to get the full benefit. The maximum credit each tax year is $2,500, lasting 4 years.
2. Lifetime Learning Credit gives up to a $2,000 tax credit on the first $10,000 of education costs if one's modified adjusted gross income is less than $90,000 in 2024 for a single filer or $180,000 for couples filing jointly. This credit is valid for unlimited years.

Individual Retirement Accounts (IRAs)

Traditional Individual Retirement Accounts

Traditional IRAs let people invest pre-tax income to grow it tax-deferred. The IRS does not tax capital gains or dividends until the beneficiary withdraws during retirement. It is then taxed at ordinary income tax rates. Individual taxpayers may donate eligible earnings. Hence, traditional IRAs are more suitable for investors in lower tax brackets at retirement than their current positions. The IRS taxes traditional IRA payouts as regular income. Distributions are available to account holders at age 59½. Some exceptions to this are as follows:

1. Buying or repairing a first home for oneself or an eligible family member (up to $10,000 per lifetime).
2. Losing functionality before distribution.
3. Utilizing assets for unpaid medical bills.
4. Including substantially equal periodic payment (SEPP) in the distribution.
5. Utilizing assets for further education, child-rearing, or medical insurance following job loss.
6. Being a military reservist on active duty for over 179 days.

Required minimum distributions (RMDs) from conventional IRAs depend on age and birthdate.

One must start taking distributions by April 1, the year after:

1. Turning 73 if one turns age 72 on or after January 1, 2023.
2. Turning 72 if one turns 70½ between January 1, 2020, and December 31, 2022.
3. Turning 70½ if one reaches that age on or before December 31, 2019.

Its features are:

1. Traditional IRA contributions are tax-deductible, unlike Roth IRA contributions.
2. Account holders should know the minimum distribution schedules and yearly contribution restrictions.
3. Before age 59½, nonqualified withdrawals from a regular IRA incur income tax and a 10% penalty.
4. The SECURE Act of 2019 lifted conventional IRA contribution age limits. No matter their age, conventional IRA account holders may contribute if they earn money.

The IRS may restrict traditional IRA contributions (hence, saving tax deduction) for having both a traditional IRA and an employer-sponsored retirement plan.

The full deduction on a standard IRA is only available to single taxpayers who participate in an employer-contributed plan such as a 401(k) or pension and have a modified adjusted gross income (MAGI) of $73,000 or less in 2023. It rises to $77,000 in 2024. Married couples filing a combined return must pay $116,000 or less in 2023 and $123,000 in 2024. IRS permits no deductions for people with MAGIs of $83,000 in 2023 ($87,000 in 2024) and married couples with $136,000 ($143,000). The deduction phases out if the filer's income is between minimum and maximum. The tax filing deadline also applies to IRA contributions. It is usually around April 15 for most taxpayers.

Other Types of IRAs

Roth IRAs

Roth IRA deposits are non-deductible, and eligible payouts are tax-free. It means you contribute after-tax cash to a Roth IRA, but investment profits are tax-free. One can withdraw taxed contributions penalty-free at any time but one must withhold until age 59½ to avoid the 10% early-withdrawal penalty. At 59½, one may take funds from the account without paying income taxes. Roth IRAs have no RMDs. Roth IRA contributions are like standard IRAs: $6,500 unless one is 50 or older and qualifies for the catch-up contribution, which boosts the cap to $7,500 in 2023, $7,000, and $8,000 in 2024. Everyone cannot contribute to a Roth IRA. Income restrictions scale off contributions as MAGI rises.

Savings Incentive Match Plans for Employees Plans (SIMPLE) IRAs and Simplified Employee Pension (SEP) IRA

Employers, self-employed, and sole traders may establish SIMPLE IRAs and SEP-IRAs, but not individuals. These IRAs work like standard ones but have more significant contribution limits and may enable business matching.

SIMPLE IRAs are retirement savings plans for most small firms with 100 or fewer workers. All workers may get a 2% retirement account contribution or a 3% matching contribution. Employees may contribute $15,500 in 2023 ($16,000 in 2024), increasing regularly to account for inflation. Retirement savings for 50 and older may add a catch-up of $3,500 to their yearly limit of $19,000 in 2023. The 2024 catch-up payment is $3,500, increasing to $19,500.

SEP-IRAs are standard IRAs with employer contributions. The instantaneous investment of employer contributions is a big advantage of this plan. The employer may avail of tax deductions for SEP plan payments and make SEP-IRA contributions to qualifying employees.

IRA Transfer

An individual retirement account (IRA) transfer involves moving money across accounts. Transfer the funds to another retirement account, brokerage account, or bank account. Transferring money to a comparable account without withdrawing it is free of penalty or taxes.

Its features are:

1. Avoid tax penalties by transferring RAs within 60 days.
2. One cannot transfer the necessary minimum distribution.
3. At 59½, one may withdraw funds from a conventional IRA without penalty.
4. The IRS regulates IRA transfers.
5. Transferring IRAs across typical accounts is straightforward. Traditional IRA holders may switch providers without a charge. Transferring a Roth IRA is the same for similar account types.
6. Traditional IRAs have the highest tax consequences if liquidated or converted to a Roth. Before putting assets in a Roth IRA, investors must pay the income taxes on the conventional IRA. Investors liquidating a traditional IRA to fund a brokerage account will also incur taxes. Accounts may accept in-kind transactions, but taxes apply.

Distribution

In finance, "distribution" usually means paying assets from a fund, account, or security. The most common account distributions involve the retirement accounts. Distributions can come from various financial products. Irrespective of the source, the distribution payment typically goes directly to the beneficiary electronically or by check *as cash*. They may include the following:

1. Mutual fund distributions: net capital gains made from the portfolio profits, dividend income, and interest earned
2. Securities: interest, capital return, or dividend
3. Tax-advantaged retirement accounts: required minimum distributions, which are compulsory withdrawals after a certain age

4. A lump-sum distribution: cash disbursement paid out all at once instead of in steady installments.

Consider the following IRS requirements when transferring an IRA:

1. Transfer all distributions except the RMD and distribution of excess contributions and associated earnings.
2. The new account must receive the transfer within 60 days.
3. Each 12-month term allows one transfer. It includes all IRA accounts, excluding trustee-to-trustee or IRA-to-IRA transfers.
4. Most IRAs and retirement accounts allow transfers.
5. One's retirement plan may not accept the transfer.

A *deed of distribution* legally transfers assets when determining the rightful receiver from the decedent's will is unobtainable.

A *lump-sum distribution* is a cash disbursement paid out together instead of in steady installments. It can come from retirement plans, earned commissions, or specific debt instruments.

A *nontaxable distribution, a return of the capital, or a non-dividend distribution* pays shareholders. It is like a dividend but symbolizes a company's capital rather than profits. It's not tax-free, despite its name. Taxations apply only when the investor sells the company's shares—non-taxable distributions lower stock value. Stockholders may get non-taxable corporate spinoff shares. Cash-value life insurance dividends are also non-taxable distributions. Notifying the IRS about the non-taxable distribution as a reduction in the cost basis of the stock is mandatory.

Nondividend distributions are generally less than the investor's basis in the shares. In the unlikely situation that the distribution exceeds the basis, the shareholder must lower their cost basis to zero and declare the excess as a capital gain on IRS Form Schedule D. Suppose the investor above gets $850 in non-taxable dividends. The first $800 of distribution reduces the cost basis to $0. If one owns the shares for less than a year, one must declare the remaining $50 as a short- or long-term capital gain. Box 3 of Form 1099-DIV reports non-taxable distributions. The form lists capital return under "Non-Dividend Distributions." Companies that pay dividends may send investors this form. Otherwise, investors can record it as an ordinary dividend. Investors may learn about reporting investment income, including non-dividend distributions, in IRS Publication 550.

Mutual Fund Distributions

Mutual funds give investors capital gains, dividends, or interest in a calendar year. Mutual funds often distribute net capital gains from profits incurred on the mutual fund's holdings sales. If a stock costs $75 and sells for $150, the capital gains are $75 less by the fund's operating expenditures. Subtracting these operational expenditures yields the distribution amount. Paying the dividends and distributions reduces the fund's share price by the total per-share distribution to shareholders. Withdrawals of distribution from the fund's assets lower the price and the net asset value.

Equity and Bond Distributions

For securities like stocks or bonds, a distribution refers to a payment of interest, principal, or dividend by the security issuer to the shareholders or bondholders. When a business makes a profit, it can reinvest the funds in the business. However, it may also pay some of the proceeds to shareholders as dividends. Sometimes, the company presents a dividend reinvestment plan, where the shareholder can apply the amount to purchase additional stock or fund shares. Without a further reinvestment plan, the funds go into the investor's account as cash.

Investors receive the income from an investment trust typically as a monthly or quarterly distribution. Thus, distributions function like stock dividends. However, distributions usually offer higher yields, sometimes as high as 10% yearly. The paid-out distributions decrease a trust's taxable income. Therefore, the income tax paid is nil or negligible.

Mutual fund owners may reinvest distributions on the ex-dividend date, which settles in one day. The amount is at the fund's net asset value. But ETF owners must wait a few business days, usually three days, to reinvest their distributions.

Retirement Account Distributions

Distributions before 59½ incur IRS penalties and regular income tax. Distributions beyond age 59½ carry no penalty, but taxpayers must pay tax on withdrawn amounts at their existing tax rate.

Roth IRAs typically require monies to stay in the account until 59½ before distribution. Account holders may take assets early after the specific years but will incur penalties if the withdrawal exceeds their contributions, or the distribution includes profits.

Other retirement funds have age limits for penalty-free withdrawals, including distributions from 403(b) and 457 plans. Some public school employees, religious organizations, and other tax-exempt entities have 403(b) plans. State and municipal governments employ 457 plans with deferred salary payments.

IRA Transfer versus Rollover

When one moves money between IRAs, one shifts money between comparable accounts. The account type doesn't change, but the institution that has the account does.

However, a rollover transfers money between account types. It involves liquidating the previous account and depositing the money into a new one. Rollovers transfer some or all of the account funds. It can be direct or indirect.

1. Direct rollover transfers cash directly from one qualified account to another qualified account, such as transferring money from a 401(k) to an IRA.
2. An indirect rollover includes paying the employee directly from a qualifying retirement account like an IRA before depositing the money into another retirement account, such as a 401(k).

Each investment firm has its own policies about charging for transfer fees. Some firms may charge for taking one's business elsewhere.

Taxation

President Abraham Lincoln signed the Revenue Act on Aug. 5, 1861, instituting the first federal income tax. He did so to fund the Civil War. All yearly earnings above $800 were taxed 3%.

The highest tax rates are in the Ivory Coast, topping the list at 60%. Finland (56.95%), Denmark (56%), Japan (55.97%), Austria (55%), Sweden (52.3%), Aruba (52%), Belgium (50%), Israel (50%), and the Netherlands (49.5%) form the other top 10 tax paying nations as of 2023.

In the US, the Internal Revenue Service (IRS) taxes the yearly incomes of individuals, businesses, trusts, and other legal organizations. Employees receive gross or net income, also known as take-home pay. Net income is the final paycheck after deducting taxes, perks, and voluntary contributions. Withheld taxes imply the firm or payer paid the government on the employee's part. An employer withholds taxes based on an employee's income and Form W-4 information.

The federal income tax applies to all taxable income, including salaries, wages, incentives, bonuses, gratuities, investments, and some unearned income. Federal income tax rates are progressive; they rise with taxable income. Tax is typically based on a fraction of the gross annual income, called the taxable income. It is adjusted gross income (AGI) minus permitted categorized or standard deductions. The IRS allows individual tax filers to take the standard deduction or itemized deductions. Mortgage interest, medical costs above 7.5% of one's AGI, and other expenses are itemized deductions.

Federal revenues fund national growth and maintenance. Some see federal tax as "rent" for people who live in a nation or a levy for resource use.

Some uses of taxed revenues are

1. Fund infrastructure maintenance, government worker pensions, and benefits
2. Social Security programs, Medicare, Medicaid, CHIP, marketplace subsidies, and "safety net" programs for low-income families
3. Payments for military and global security

4. Enhance education, health, agriculture, utilities, and public transportation.
5. Space exploration
6. Help catastrophe victims

Types

Types of taxation are

1. Capital gains taxes: Personal items and investments, including stocks, houses, bonds, vehicles, and jewelry, are subject to capital gains taxes.
2. Income taxes: Individuals pay income taxes on their earnings, investments, and salaries.
3. Corporate taxes: Businesses pay corporate income tax. To stimulate economic development, most countries tax corporations below 30%.
4. Payroll taxes: Employees pay payroll taxes for social security funds. The employer automatically deducts and pays payroll taxes on behalf of the employee. The highest payroll taxes in the US are 12.4% for Social Security and 2.9% for Medicare, totaling 15.3%. The employer pays 7.65% of the tax rate or half of the payroll taxes.
5. Property taxes: Most property taxes apply to land and buildings. Local state governments rely on them for income. Over 70% of municipal taxes come from property taxes. Property taxes help fund fire departments, schools, roads, security, and emergency medical services.

Classes

Classifying taxes is by the form of payment, individuals bearing the tax burden, and the amount of burden transfer.

1. Direct: Individuals pay direct taxes on their wealth, expenses, or net income. Net worth taxes are based on the taxpayer's assets minus liabilities, whereas expenditure taxes are on incomes not saved.
2. Indirect: Indirect taxes apply to imports, exports, manufacturing, and consumption. Value-added, legal transactions, manufacturing, and import taxes are examples.

Taxable Income

1. Earned income

   a. Wages: salary or hourly pay
   b. Business income/income from operations
   c. Pensions and other retirement benefits
   d. Sick pay and other fringe benefits
   e. Self-employment income

2. Unearned income comes from passive activities like:

   a. Income from dividends, interest, and valued assets sold throughout the year
   b. Canceled debts
   c. Unemployment
   d. Disability payments
   e. Strike benefits
   f. Lottery payouts
   g. Royalties or residual income
   h. Staking rewards or airdropped digital currency
   i. Social Security payments are not gross income. The IRS considers benefits part of the combined income. AGI, nontaxable interest, and half of Social Security benefits comprise combined income. A 50% tax on benefits is payable for income ranges of $25,000–$34,000. If the total income exceeds $34,000, 85% of the benefits can be taxed.

Not all companies disclose revenue as taxable income on their taxes. Instead, they calculate firm income by subtracting expenditures from revenue. They determine taxable income by subtracting deductions. Taxable income determines tax brackets and marginal tax rates. Tax brackets signify the income ranges to which specific tax rates apply. Federal income tax rates for 2024 vary from 10% to 37% and start at certain income levels.

Payment of marginal tax is fixed on an individual's highest dollar of income., which falls into the highest tax bracket. Therefore, the marginal tax rate will likely be greater than one's effective tax rate—the average rate one pays on all one's income. This method of taxation is progressive taxation. It attempts to tax people depending on their wages, with lower rates for those with lower incomes. Annually, federal income tax is due on April 15. The day may change if April 15 is a weekend or for other causes.

Sources of taxation include

1. Employee compensation and fringe benefits
2. Income from investments and businesses
3. Partnership income
4. S-corporation income
5. Royalties
6. Barters
7. Digital currencies

Examples of nontaxable income include

1. Religious or charitable organization earnings that are eventually given back to that organization
2. Employee achievement award under specific conditions
3. Life insurance benefit gained by a beneficiary, except for the estate tax

Besides the Federal government, some states in the US charge taxes. State governments like Alaska, Florida, Nevada, South Dakota, Tennessee, Texas, and Wyoming have no income taxes in 2023. New Hampshire taxes dividends and interest alone, although it will eliminate them by 2027.

Tax Filing

The IRS receives federal income taxes via the Department of Treasury's forms. Form 1040, the main federal income tax form, gathers personal information and income and tax benefit activities for the year. Form 1040 varies by taxpayer behavior from the previous year.

Tax Reduction

A greater tax burden might result from a taxable income at year's end. The standard deduction on the return of taxes lowers this number for most individuals. Alternatively, itemize and include all deductions. Contributing to a 401(k), individual retirement account, health savings account, and flexible spending account are other ways of tax reduction.

Tax credits lower a taxpayer's tax bill legally. A taxpayer may directly lower their tax credit amounts after calculating a taxpayer's tax liability. Suppose a taxpayer with one child is eligible for the Child Tax Credit. Consider this person's taxable income is $45,000, and tax liability is $4,500. The Child Tax Credit cuts taxes from $4,500 to $2,900. Instead of applying to $50,000, the Child Tax Credit applies directly to the tax liability. The highest tax credits are for legislative incentives for particular taxpayers. For instance, low-income people get tax credits from the Earned Income Tax Credit, while students in higher education receive tax credits from the American Opportunity Tax Credit and Lifetime Learning Credit. Parents take the help of the Child and Dependent Care Credit.

Some Federal *tax credits are nonrefundable*. If they decrease the tax burden to $0, a refund or further benefit from an unused credit component may not be obtained. For instance, the Adoption Tax Credit is a nonrefundable tax credit that lowers taxpayers' tax burden to zero, meaning they do not pay taxes.

Conversely, a *refundable tax credit* can give back money. It may decrease a taxpayer's burden to zero or even result in a tax refund. Thus, a $250 for $750 in taxes that qualifies for a $1,000 refundable tax credit is the tax refund for an individual under refundable tax.

Taxation on Capital Gains and Dividends

Capital gains tax rates are less than income tax rates, depending on how long the seller held the item. Ordinary income rates apply to short-term capital gains for assets held less than a year. Long-term capital gains apply for retaining an investment for more than a year. These rates are 0%, 15%, or 20%, depending on income. Capital losses may cut effective taxes by offsetting capital gains in a tax year. Short-term and long-term losses may counter short-term and long-term profits, respectively.

A company's share of the profits that regularly pass to the shareholders comprises ordinary dividends. Regular dividend income is a major benefit of owning stocks, also known as equities. Dividends become "qualified" if they fulfill certain conditions. The capital gains rate applies to qualifying dividends, whereas ordinary dividends are taxed as regular income. An American or qualifying foreign corporation must be eligible for a qualified dividend provision, and the IRS must not label it as an unqualified dividend. Also, it must satisfy a holding period (Kurt, 2023).

1. Common stock and dividend-paying mutual funds: 60 days
2. Preferred stock: 90 days

Domestic or international corporations that pay qualified dividends must hold them for at least 61 days out of the 121 days, starting 60 days before the ex-dividend date. Ex-dividend stocks have no dividend rights. The corporation trades without its next dividend payout on the "ex-date" or ex-dividend date. Investors purchasing the shares on the ex-dividend date or later will not get the dividend but will receive the dividend the day before the ex-dividend date.

In 2003, the Jobs and Growth Tax Relief Reconciliation Act cut the maximum long-term capital gains tax rate from 20% to 15% and set a 5% rate for individuals in the 10% and 15% regular income tax categories. In 2005, the Tax Increase Prevention and Reconciliation Act (TIPRA) extended some provisions under the 2003 tax laws until 2010. It also cut the tax rate on long-term capital gains and qualifying dividends from 5% to 0% for low-to-middle-income taxpayers in the 10% and 15% ordinary income tax band.

The 2010 legislation, Tax Relief, Unemployment Insurance Reauthorization, and Job Creation Act extended these protections for two years. In 2013, the legislation American Taxpayer Relief Act of 2012 made qualified dividends permanent and added a 20% income tax rate to a newly established bracket, making it the highest tax bracket (signed Jan. 2, 2013). The IRS may change all tax bands for inflation annually.

The maximum tax rate for qualified and ordinary dividends in 2021 is 20% and

37%. President Trump's 2017 legislation, the Tax Cuts and Jobs Act, had little impact on dividend and capital gains taxes.

Year	Income	Capital gains tax rate
2022	$41,675 or less	0%
2023	$44,625	0%
2022	$459,750 or less	15%
2023	$492,300 or less	15%
2022	$459,750	20%
2023	$492,300	20%

Realized vs. Unrealized Profits

Realized profits: Realized profits are cash-converted gains. To benefit from an investment, the investor must get cash and not just see the market price rise without selling. If an investor holds 1,000 common shares of ABC Business and the company pays a $0.60 per share cash dividend, the investor should earn $600 in cash, which is unwashed by market movements. The US taxes only realized earnings as short-term capital gains tax that is taxed at ordinary income rates and long-term capital gains tax at 0%, 15%, or 20% rates depending on filing status and total income.

Unrealized profits: If the investor doesn't realize their profit, they need not report it as income. Investors may delay taxable income for a year or more by holding their shares instead of selling. Conversely, investors may claim realized losses as capital losses to offset capital gains; paper losses do not have this value. Unrealized losses or gains are also called paper losses or gains. An unrealized gain is an item already invested in that has appreciated but has yet to be sold. Thus, these value changes only show "on paper" in consumer brokerage or account statements.

The well-known concept of loss aversion in behavioral finance suggests that individuals cling to losing prospects too long because the psychological anguish of losing is hard to endure. Thus, losing $100 hurts more than finding it. As they say, "losses loomed larger than gains." Investors call this the *disposal effect*. Thus, investors hold losing equities too long and sell winners too soon.

Wash Sales

Investors buy securities 30 days before or 30 days after selling a comparable asset, making a wash sale. Many nations enable investors to deduct a certain percentage of capital losses from their income. In the US, investors can recover $3,000 or the net loss, whichever is less. Capital losses above $3,000 can be rolled over into the next financial year. The investors devised a way to sell and purchase a losing investment again quickly. It enabled them to claim a capital loss and reduce taxes.

The IRS proposed the wash sale rule to discourage people from reducing their tax obligations. The UK calls the practice bed-and-breakfasting, and its tax requirements are identical to the Wash Sale Rule. The legislation prohibits reporting losses from securities sales if an investor acquires it within 30 days after selling it.

Tax on Inherited and Gifted Shares

Inherited Shares

The US has taxed heirs' asset transfers since the 1916 Revenue Act, which supplemented the income tax to support World War I. Proponents said estate taxation may provide much-needed revenue and prevent wealth concentration. Estate tax opponents term it the "Death Tax" and say wealth taxation is unfair after income tax. The debate about inheritance taxes is contentious. However, capital gain taxes cover inherited stock. Selling inherited assets can trigger capital gains taxes.

It contrasts with yearly income taxes. The stepped-up basis exemption advocates taxing capital gains less than income to encourage consumer spending and economic investment. Benefactors should avoid selling stock they want to leave to their heirs during their lifetimes since heirs won't have to pay capital gains taxes on unsold stock.

1. The inherited stock has better tax advantages than the gifted stock. All inherited stock is long-term property.
2. After the original shareholder dies, heirs get inherited stocks.
3. An increase in a stock's value between the decedent's purchase and death is not taxed.

4. The initial value or original cost basis during the purchase does not pertain to the valuation of the inherited stock.
5. A recipient inherits a stock at a stepped-up cost basis depending on the security's value during the inheritance date.

Gifted Shares

The IRS permits individuals to contribute up to $16,000 per person without reporting or paying gift taxes in 2022. It rises to $17,000 in 2023; however, this tax ranges from 18% to 40% on a sliding scale. Based on the measure of the taxable gift, it only applies when donations surpass the lifetime gift tax immunity of $12.06 million in 2022 and $12.92 million in 2023. Gifts between spouses are unlimited. Gifts might be cash, stocks, bonds, or other valuables.

1. Gifted stocks are shares given as a gift to another.
2. Gifting stocks may save taxes, but consult an adviser.
3. Gifted equities are transferred via a brokerage account or a transfer on death (TOD) arrangement.
4. For taxation, the cost basis is their fair market value during offering and sale.
5. The IRS limits the value of gifts of stocks permitted without reporting or taxing them.

Consider capital gains tax obligations for donating stocks. Selling the stock and gifting the money would require reporting capital gains and paying tax after deducting its cost basis. Gifting the shares may be worthwhile, especially if the receiver has a reduced tax rate.

The donee (recipient) accepts share cost basis and holding duration. Thus, a donee must pay long-term capital gains taxes on a $5,000 profit if they sell $12,000 assets the donor bought five years earlier for $7,000. If the recipient sells donated stock that depreciates, the loss equals the transfer date's fair market value.

The same rules apply to child gifts. When selling gifted shares, the donee kid pays less capital gains taxes if they make little or no money. However, the Kiddie tax applies to values less than $2,300. Anything above this is taxed at the guardian's rate.

Cost Basis

Cost basis is an asset's value, generally its purchase price adjusted for dividends, splits, and return of capital distributions. It serves tax purposes and determines the capital gain. Capital gain is the difference between the asset's cost basis and market value. Using the correct cost basis (tax basis) is crucial for reinvesting dividends and capital gains instead of receiving cash. Reinvesting dividends raises an investment's tax basis, which must be accounted for to report lower capital gain and pay less tax. Cost basis may also indicate the gap between a commodity's cash and futures prices.

Stock heirs for inherited securities cannot recover damages incurred while the original owner was alive. Thus, if a deceased bought a share of stock for $100 and it dropped to $35 by the time they died, an heir's cost basis would be $35. The $65 loss cannot be employed to offset profits from other assets. For tax purposes, the cost basis of inherited stock is the value at the time of the original owner's death, not the original purchase price. The stock inheritor only pays taxes on the price change between inheritance and sale (Bloomenthal, 2023).

Gift Tax

Individual taxpayers who transfer property to others without obtaining considerable return value are subject to a gift tax by the IRS. Cash, real estate, and other things may be gifted. The IRS restricts gifting. Reporting and applying any amount above this level for lifetime gift tax exemption is mandatory. The gift tax applies once this value is surpassed, even when the transfer was not intended to be a gift.

1. Hence, all gifts are notifiable whether or not they incur gift tax. Donors must file Form 709: United States donation (and Generation-Skipping Transfer) Tax Return. This form is attached to the yearly tax return by the tax filing date, usually April 15, the year after the gift was made.

2. Two strategies to avoid gift tax are gift splitting, gifts given in trust, and some 529 plans.

   a. Gift splits: Married people double their gifts. The annual exclusion application means that each spouse may give $18,000 in 2024 to the same beneficiary even if they file a combined tax return. Effectively, married couples may double their tax-free gift to one individual. Gift splitting lets wealthy families provide significant yearly contributions to children, grandkids, and others. Another donation, such as tuition to a grandchild's school or college, is free from the gift tax. A *generation-skipping transfer tax* (GSTT) of 40% is charged when a gift over a specific amount is gifted to anyone 37½ years younger than the donor. The limit is the lifetime exclusion, which is $13.61 million for 2024.

   b. Gifts to trust: The gift exclusion tax never applies to money distributed by gift in trust conveyances. Creating a private trust to collect and distribute contributions beyond the yearly exclusion lets donors contribute more without incurring taxes. The Crummey trust is noteworthy. The beneficiary may withdraw assets under this trust within 90 days or six months. It gives the recipient a current stake in the trust, which the IRS considers a nontaxable gift. The beneficiary may only withdraw the amount equal to the gift sum.

   c. College savings plan: Certain 529 college savings plan contributions allow individuals to contribute more than the yearly exclusion without lowering their lifetime gift tax exemption. Sometimes, individuals can record an enormous gift spread across five years on the tax return and submit it annually. However, they cannot give the same person any further gifts during this time. Doing so will apply to their lifetime exclusion.

Items considered gifts	Items not considered gifts
Cash	Educational expenditures for another individual
Securities	Medical costs for another person
Real estate and vehicles	Gifts made to a spouse
Art	Gifts and donations to political establishments

Property is a gift if it has worth. Transference of inherited property does not incur much compensation.

1. Gift tax rates vary from 18% to 40%, depending on the gift amount.
2. If securities are complex to evaluate, their fair market value (FMV) is used to calculate the tax burden.
3. For American spouses, limitless gifted amounts are tax-free. The yearly adjusted value of tax-free gifts for non-American spouses is $185,000 in 2024.

Chapter Five: Client Accounts and Margin Trading

This chapter thoroughly guides the complexities of client accounts, margin trading, and the associated regulatory requirements. It will help in informed decision-making.

Margin Accounts

Investors utilize margin accounts to borrow money to buy securities. Investors must pay monthly interest on brokerage loans. A margin-approved account lets customers buy additional financial instruments like stocks and bonds. Brokers may trade stocks using margin accounts, commonly known as loan accounts.

Margin account lending began to finance railroads in the late 1800s. By 1920, investors had to deposit a minimal amount to get credit from brokers. Over time, brokerages have required investors to have a credit limit of up to 50% of their equity. Brokerages must have a credit limit of at least 25% of investor equity value under Federal Reserve Regulation T.

Federal and FINRA laws control how FINRA member firms (brokers) may offer credit for securities transactions. For certain securities, the purchaser must deposit 100% of the purchase amount. These securities are not available on margin, but they can be held in margin accounts. Under Federal Reserve Board Regulation T (Reg T), brokers may lend clients up to 50% of the margin equity security's purchase price for new transactions.

FINRA's margin regulation, 4210, adds initial margin requirements for instruments like corporate bonds that Reg T does not prescribe. Regulation T only sets the initial margin requirements on equity securities. Rule 4210 further limits account losses with maintenance obligations. Customers must deposit more collateral or sell holdings if an account falls below these limitations (a "margin deficiency"). Importantly, brokers may liquidate accounts at any moment to fix a margin shortage. Margin loans have no repayment schedule, but the account value must be over the maintenance margin.

Financial authorities like FINRA, SEC, and Federal Reserve impose maintenance margins. Individual brokerages may establish their minimum balance requirements, generally greater than financial authorities'.

The FINRA rules controlling margin accounts are as follows:

1. FINRA Rule 4210: FINRA Rule 4210 (Margin Requirements) defines the margin requirements that specify the sum of collateral clients must maintain in their margin accounts, including strategy-based and portfolio margin accounts. The rule explains the margin requirements for equity and fixed-income securities, options, warrants, and security futures. The interpretations of Rule 4210 explain the rule, state the rule's actual text, and publish it. These guide and assist people in better understanding the application of the rule.
2. FINRA Rule 4220: Daily log of obligatory margin
3. FINRA Rule 4230: Request submission for time extensions is required under Regulation T and SEA Rule 15c3-3. FINRA Rule 4230 allows member firms to solicit further time to concede with the payment term for purchases and margin shortcomings as demanded by Regulation T. The rule also enables member firms to request more time for particular short security requirements.
4. FINRA Rule 4240: Security-based swap margin necessities
5. FINRA Rule 4521 mandates that member firms holding customer margin accounts must use the customer margin balance form to submit to FINRA numbers, which FINRA publishes in aggregate form on the margin statistics page. The numbers are:

    a. Total debit balances in securities margin accounts
    b. Free credit balances in all cash accounts.

c. The settlement date for all securities margin accounts is on the final business day of the month.

Portfolio Margining

Portfolio margining establishes margin requirements for an account based on the highest expected net loss of all holdings in a group of connected securities, such as a stock and options that reference it. The calculation uses computer modeling to do risk analysis utilizing numerous pricing scenarios to estimate prospective profits or losses of investments given price fluctuations. Thus, the margin needed is the largest loss a portfolio would experience if its components change by a defined amount.

Covered Agency Transaction Margin

The modified margin requirements for Covered Agency Transactions under SR-FINRA-2021-010 will take effect on May 22, 2024. Under amended Rule 4210(e)(2)(H)(i)b., "Covered Agency Transactions" are (1) To Be Announced (TBA) transactions (including flexible rate mortgage transactions) with settlement dates later than T+1, (2) Specified Pool Transactions with settlement dates later than T+1, and (3) Collateralized Mortgage Obligations (CMO) transactions issued in compliance with a program of an agency or Government-Sponsored Enterprise (GSE), with settlement dates after T+3.

Disclosure Statements on Margin Requirements

According to FINRA Rule 2264 (Margin Disclosure Statement), no member may open a margin account, as stated in Regulation T, for or in the name of a non-institutional customer without first providing the margin disclosure statement to the customer in a separate document, in paper or electronic form. Any member that allows non-institutional consumers to create accounts or trade securities online must prominently display the margin disclosure statement on its website.

FINRA Rule 4210(g) requires members to provide consumers with a written disclosure statement explaining portfolio margining's risks on or before the first portfolio margin account transaction.

All portfolio margin account owners must sign a disclosure statement acknowledgment, certifying they have read and understood it. Additionally, customers must state that they accept their portfolio margin account conditions. Members must save this signed acknowledgment and receipt date. FINRA furnishes more details in Regulatory Notice 08-09.

Regulation T and Margin Account

Regulation T regulates investors' cash accounts and the credit amount that brokerage companies and dealers may furnish the customers for purchasing securities. According to Regulation T, investors can take loans up to 50% of the purchase price of stocks using a broker or dealer loan. Cash must cover the remaining 50%. Investors seeking to buy securities using broker-dealer credit must apply for a margin account.

The Board of Governors of the Federal Reserve System created Regulation T to govern broker-dealer credit and cash accounts. Investors with cash accounts cannot borrow from broker-dealers and must pay for securities with cash. Investors can apply for credit to buy assets through margin accounts. Credit purchases might expose investors to bigger losses than cash purchases. Hence, the Federal Reserve Board restricted borrowing to 50% of the purchase price of securities. The 50% initial margin sets a minimum borrowing threshold during acquisition. Brokers may have higher criteria over 50%.

Like any loan, investors who purchase shares on margin must repay the loan plus interest, which varies by brokerage company. Investors pay monthly principal interest on their brokerage accounts. The yearly margin interest rate is what investors pay on margin accounts and loans. Margin interest rates vary per brokerage. Margin account rates are 3% to 4%, greater than home equity line of credit (HELOC) rates. Short-term margin account investments may have a beneficial interest rate. The cost of accumulated interest may diminish returns if customers utilize margin accounts often.

The uses of margin accounts are:

1. A brokerage company lends cash to buy shares on margin using an account as collateral. Margin accounts allow investors to trade on margin.
2. Selling non-owned stocks (shorting) also requires margin accounts. The stockbroker loans the shares to sell.
3. Many options trading tactics need a margin account.

Freeriding

While regulating margin was its primary purpose, Regulation T regulated cash account transactions. Securities settlements and cash payments to vendors of the securities take up to two days. Thus, an investor may purchase and sell the same stocks before paying with cash. Called freeriding, it is an illegal action under Reg T.

Margin Call

The three methods to get a margin call:

1. Trading beyond the account's purchasing capacity.
2. The margin account loses value.
3. The broker increases house maintenance margin necessities.

Trading Beyond an Account's Purchasing Capacity

General Federal Reserve Board Regulation T (Reg T) allows enterprises to initially lend customers up to 50% of the acquisition price of an eligible stock. A business may restrict margin purchases or ownership of specific securities. This may include equities that don't trade on a national exchange like the NYSE or Nasdaq and stocks the business feels are prone to substantial daily price movements.

Suppose you have $2,000 purchasing power and purchase $10,000 of stock on margin, the company will lend you 50% of the price. Reg T allows "one payment period," four business days (3 days from May 28, 2024) from the transaction date, to fulfill the initial margin requirement of $4,000, 50% of $8,000 (the entire purchase price minus the purchasing power). However, the business may decrease the payment time and ask for a bigger initial margin.

Whether the stock you bought on leverage rises or falls, you'll receive a margin call asking for a $4,000 payment if you miss this date. The company may extend the deadline (an extension) in extreme situations, but they are not compelled to. The company must liquidate your account assets without a deposit and an extension. The business may sell your margin-purchased shares or other account assets.

The Margin Account Loses Value

It is unnecessary to deposit cash to open a margin account. However, FINRA rules require an account to have a value of at least $2,000 before the investor can engage in margin trading. Alternatively, the FINRA requires a 100% deposit equal to 100% of the purchase price of the securities the investors want to buy on margin. The investor may get a margin call if the account equity falls below firm or FINRA maintenance margin requirements. Margin trading requires a minimum account balance. Some firms employ "account equity" and "liquidation value" to characterize margin account value.

FINRA requires a "maintenance" margin on client margin accounts in addition to Reg T. Generally, a margin account customer's equity cannot fall below 25% of the market value of the long securities (completely paid for).

Raising House Margin Requirements

Firms may also establish "house" margin requirements greater than Reg T or FINRA and exchange regulations. For example, a business may set the maintenance margin at 30% or 40% of an account's holdings' market value. Companies might sometimes raise house requirements without prior warning.

The company can raise house margin requirements on an account's security or group of securities. When a business goes bankrupt, is delisted from the securities exchange, or has huge daily price movements (volatility), its house margin needs may rise. Companies may also impose greater house requirements for particular stock groups in specific industries.

A business isn't obligated to inform if an account equity falls below minimal maintenance. Firms may sell assets in the margin account to satisfy a margin call without issuing a margin call and may sell enough securities to pay off the margin debt. Also, businesses don't require the account holder's permission to pick which securities or assets to sell to fulfill margin calls.

Fulfilling The Margin Call

1. Deposit the margin call amount.
2. Deposit margin-eligible investments. Securities must be worth more than the margin call to fulfill it. For a $6,000 house margin call and a stock in another account with a 40% house requirement, the investor needs to deposit $10,000 of that stock to fulfill the house margin call (Know What Triggers a Margin Call, 2023).

   a. The formula for deriving the deposit amount is

      i. Margin call amount / (100% less than the margin requirement %). In the example, the margin call amount = $6,000 / .6 = $10,000

3. Selling account securities. The securities sold may be worth much more than the call. For a $6,000 house margin call and selling a security with a 40% house requirement, an individual must sell $15,000 to fulfill the call.

   a. The formula for deriving the selling amount is

      i. Margin call amount/the margin provision %, or 6,000 / .4 = $15,000

Individual Accounts

Account holders sign bank contracts and control the money in their accounts. Choosing an account's ownership may have consequences and duties. Any loan debt will make an account holder responsible for taxes.

Joint and several or indistinct bank account ownership means an account with more than one holder where any holder may utilize the money without the others' permission. If it needs authorization, it will be joint or joint and several. It will be subordinate if each owner has a distinct status. The person in first position doesn't require anybody else's permission to operate, but the person in second place needs authorization from the first individual, and so forth.

After notifying the bank with the death certificate, the heirs will take over the rights and responsibilities of a deceased account holder's accounts. The account balance will be frozen until the inheritance is managed. If account ownership is unclear, other owners can manage it. If one joint owner dies, the others need the consent of heirs.

Authorized Signatory

One may approve an individual holding authorized activity on one's account by writing to the bank branch and giving a photocopy of the identification card. Authorized individuals and proxies may be added after the account is established, but not account holders.

If the holder is an authorized signatory of the bank account, the signatory will have authorized them to spend the money on their behalf, but they will not control the account or its assets. The authorized individual with a signature to manage the account on behalf of those they represent may utilize the balance, issue checks, transfer funds, and seek bank information without the account holder's approval. However, not being the holder will not have tax ramifications, and the person in question cannot make applications for debit or credit cards in their name, cancel any of the represented individual's financial products, or block or amend an account or product after their death.

Payable on Death (POD) and Transfer on Death Accounts (TOD)

Banks and clients may designate beneficiaries to receive assets after death without probate via a "payable on death" (POD) designation. Certificates of deposit (CDs) and bank accounts are PODs, whereas stocks, bonds, deeds, and other assets are TODs.

The transfer on death (TOD) classification enables someone to inherit assets from a donor without probate. Account holders or security owners may define the proportion of assets each individual gets using a TOD designation, helping the executor divide assets after death. Brokerage accounts, stocks, bonds, and other investments usually include a transfer on death designation. Thus, A transfer on death is an instrument that transfers the control of specific accounts and assets to someone (beneficiary). A beneficiary is one designated to receive something of value.

Uses

1. Transfer on death registrations prevents identified beneficiaries from accessing or controlling a person's assets while they are alive.
2. Before the owner's death, TOD beneficiaries can't access assets.
3. The brokerage needs the proper documentation to transfer assets and execute a TOD.

Disadvantages

1. Transfer on death designations prevent probate, but estate, capital gains, and inheritance taxes apply.
2. TOD accounts' assets remain part of the deceased's inheritance. Creditors might demand repayment before beneficiaries can access assets.

Needed Paperwork and New Account

After receiving notifications of an account holder's death, the brokerage company requires a death certificate, current court letter of appointment, stock power of attorney, affidavit of domicile, or other verification. The needed paperwork is determined by whether the account is single or joint, whether one or both holders are dead, or whether the trustee or grantor is deceased.

The beneficiary usually receives the deceased's stocks and money in a new account. The securities cannot be operated or used before the account is opened and legal possession is established. The beneficiary must apply to open a new account and supply personal information. This information helps brokers understand the account owner (beneficiary), fulfill their financial demands, and comply with laws.

Partnership Accounts

Two or more persons join a partnership to run a business and split earnings. There are several kinds of partnerships. Partners in a partnership firm share obligations and earnings equally, which is called a general partnership. A partnership agreement includes profit sharing. A partnership agreement should contain an expulsion provision stating the reasons for ousting a partner.

But in others, they have limited responsibility. Accountants, attorneys, and architects often form limited liability partnerships (LLPs). In the event of a malpractice lawsuit, this structure restricts partners' personal culpability, protecting other partners' assets. Some legal and accounting companies distinguish equity and salaried partners. The latter is senior to associates but without ownership. The firm's profitability determines its bonuses.

Limited partnerships combine general and limited liability partnerships. At least one general partner must be personally liable for partnership obligations. At least one silent partner has a limited responsibility for the investment. A silent partner often does not engage in the management or daily operations of the partnership.

The unusually termed limited liability partnership is new and uncommon. This limited partnership better protects general partners.

The law does not define partnerships, but the Internal Revenue Code (Chapter 1, Subchapter K) details their federal tax status. A partnership does not pay income tax; the burden passes to partners, who are not employees for tax purposes. Partnerships may have better tax treatment than corporations. Thus, corporate earnings and shareholder dividends are taxed. However, partnership earnings are not double-taxed.

Institutional Accounts

Institutional investors invest money for others. Examples include pensions, insurance, and mutual funds. Institutional investors purchase and sell large blocks of stocks, bonds, and other assets, making them Wall Street whales. The group is also considered more sophisticated than regular investors and may have fewer rules. Institutional investors may research more investment choices than individual investors.

These institutions drive supply and demand in securities markets; they trade heavily on important exchanges and affect asset prices. Nearly 90% of stock trading is by institutions. Retail investors typically check institutional investors' SEC filings to decide which stocks to purchase because institutional investors may impact markets. Thus, some investors try to emulate institutional purchasing by adopting the same positions as "smart money."

Retail and institutional investors trade bonds, options, commodities, currencies, futures, and stocks. Retail investors purchase and sell stocks in 100-share rounds, whereas institutional investors buy and sell in 10,000-share blocks. Because it may violate securities regulations, institutional investors avoid obtaining a substantial proportion of firm ownership. Diversified mutual funds, closed-end funds, and ETFs may only hold a certain proportion of a company's voting shares.

Institutional investors make investments for others. Insight and analytical data from Institutional Shareholder Services (ISS) providers help them make crucial shareholder decisions. Pension funds, mutual funds, insurance companies, university endowments, and sovereign wealth funds are institutional investors. The six types of institutional investors are:

1. Endowment funds
2. Commercial banks

3. Mutual funds
4. Hedge funds
5. Pension funds
6. Insurance companies

Accredited investors, often sophisticated investors, have the expertise or resources to make hazardous bets that the public cannot. Accredited investors in the US must have a net worth of $1 million, excluding their principal residence.

Institutional Commingled Fund

Institutional commingled funds, like mutual funds, pool assets and are unlisted to retail investors and the public. These commingled funds combine asset accounts to save expenses. Pension funds, insurance policies, and retirement plans are some examples. Banks or trust companies handle these funds, which gives several benefits:

1. Scale economies
2. Providing institutional investors with a diverse portfolio
3. Lower costs
4. Possibly higher returns

Separate Accounts

Separate accounts are registered investment advisors (RIA)-managed portfolios. It meets institutional investor requirements. Institutional investors employ an investment manager or asset management business to handle their portfolio directly, separated from pooled funds like mutual and commingled funds.

Prime Brokerage

Investment banks and major clients, like hedge funds, sign prime brokerage agreements. In return for prime brokerage fees, the bank offers customers unique services. Regular investors can't get this bargain but don't need it either. Efficient stock brokers satisfy the needs of most investors. Prime brokerage agreements help an extensive clientele that requires various financial services.

They serve the following functions:

1. Holding client securities for protection
2. Securities and cash loans
3. Reporting of finances
4. Capital introductions
5. Consulting on risk management
6. Operational help (Hedge funds can outsource securities trading)

Clients pay fees for premium brokerage. Legally, premium brokerage services need $500,000 in equity. Clients often have $50 million or more equity. Several variables determine the quantity, including:

1. Total services
2. Volume of transactions
3. Funds borrowed for margin financing
4. Total short-traded securities borrowed

Six big brokers that offer prime brokerage services:

1. Goldman Sachs
2. Bank of America Merrill Lynch
3. J.P. Morgan
4. Morgan Stanley
5. Citigroup
6. Charles Schwab

Chapter Six: Practice Test I

You have three hours to complete the 125 questions in this test.

1.   Which is true about a Regulation D offering?

   A. No more than 55 unaccredited investors per year are eligible.
   B. No more than 50 unaccredited investors per year are eligible.
   C. It is a private placement.
   D. It is a public placement.

2.   Under the Securities Act of 1933, which can the SEC authorize?

   A. New issues of common stock
   B. Stop orders review
   C. Registration statements

      i.   A and B
      ii.   B and C
      iii. A and C
      iv.   All of the above

3.   Which of the following may not occur during the cooling-off period?

   A. Having a due diligence meeting
   B. Obtaining indications of interest
   C. The publishing of a tombstone ad

D. Soliciting sales of the new security

4.   What must ADec Corporation do to have a public offering of common stock?

A. Issue a prospectus.
B. Publish a tombstone advertisement.
C. Register the securities with the SEC.

   i.   A and B
   ii.   B and C
   iii. A and C
   iv.   A, B, and C

5.   A tombstone ad includes all of the following names EXCEPT:

A. Selling group members
B. Syndicate members
C. The syndicate manager
D. The issuer

6.   Isabel is a new client. At 82, her monthly expenses exceed her social security. She owns barely $5,000 in cash besides $4000 in Class B Mutual Funds. Which solution may help Maria reinvest fund income and capital gains?

A. Raise Large-cap holdings, such as S&P 500 companies.
B. Alter dividend and capital gains reinvestment to cash.
C. Trade out of her Class B bond mutual funds and buy ETFs.
D. Liquidate the Class B Mutual Funds and purchase safe Municipal Bonds.

7.   Zzow, Inc. has filed a registration statement and is currently in the cooling-off period. A broker-dealer is the lead underwriter for Zzow and is in the process of taking indications of interest. Which two of the following are TRUE regarding indications of interest?

A. They are binding on Zzow.
B. They are binding on clients.

C. They are not binding on Zzow.
D. They are not binding on clients.

    i.   A and B
   ii.   C and D
  iii.   A and D
   iv.   B and C

8.   Which are state securities registrations?

A. Filing
B. Communication
C. Qualification
D. Coordination

    i.   A, C, and D
   ii.   A, C, and D
  iii.   A, B, and C
   iv.   A, B, C, and D

9.   Which state securities registrations are used for established companies that have previously sold securities in the state?

A. Notification
B. Coordination
C. Indemnification
D. Qualification

10.   Which type of mandatory state securities registration is used for securities exempt from SEC registration?

A. Notification
B. Coordination
C. Indemnification
D. Qualification

11.   The managing underwriter may determine all of the following EXCEPT:

   A. The takedown
   B. The public offering price
   C. The effective date
   D. Order allocation

12.   What does it mean when the SEC rules that an offering has become effective?

   A. The SEC has approved the issue.
   B. The SEC has cleared the issue.
   C. The SEC has verified the accuracy of the information provided on the registration statement.
   D. All of the above.

13.   Which of the following securities acts covers the registration and disclosure requirements of new issues?

   A. The Securities Act of 1933.
   B. The Securities Exchange Act of 1934.
   C. The Trust Indenture Act of 1939.
   D. All of the above

14.   Which of the following are covered under the Securities and Exchange Act 1934?

   A. Margin accounts
   B. Trust indentures
   C. Proxies
   D. Short sales

      i.   A, B, and C
      ii. B and D
      iii. C and D
      iv. A, C, and D

15. Per the Trust Indenture Act of 1939, what is the maximum value for corporate bond issues that can be offered to investors without an indenture?

    A. $5 million
    B. $10 million
    C. $50 million
    D. $75 million

16. What is the main function of an investment banker?

    A. Advise an issuer on how to raise capital.
    B. Sell securities to raise capital for issuers.
    C. Assist issuers to follow the Securities Act of 1933.
    D. All of the above.

17. Which is NOT TRUE concerning Eurodollar deposits?

    A. They pay a higher interest rate than US banks.
    B. The Federal Reserve Board (FRB) determines the interest rate.
    C. The deposit is denominated in US dollars but held in foreign banks.
    D. The risk is higher than US bank deposits.

18. Which is a money market instrument?

    A. Short-term debt
    B. Long-term debt
    C. Common stock
    D. Preferred stock

19. A small-time investor is interested in purchasing negotiable CDs. What is the minimum denomination for negotiable CDs?

    A. $25,000
    B. $50,000
    C. $100,000
    D. $500,000

20. When recommending collateralized debt obligations (CDOs) to one of your clients, you may state which of the following?

    A. The loans that determine the value of the CDOs are liquid.
    B. CDOs have tranches that have different forms of prepayment and extension risk.
    C. CDOs are not suitable for all investors.
    D. They represent the securitization of non-mortgage loans, including credit cards and auto loans.

    i.   A only
    ii. A and C
    iii. B and D
    iv. B, C, and D

21. Which is not valid for collateralized debt obligations?

    A. They are asset-backed securities.
    B. They are always backed by mortgages.
    C. They are backed by credit cards, auto loans, etc.
    D. They are liquid investments

22. While recommending to a client interested in collateralized mortgage obligations (CMOs), which of the following can you compare them to?

    A. Certificates of deposit
    B. Mortgage bonds
    C. Other CMOs only
    D. Federal National Mortgage Association (FNMAs)

23. Which are companion tranches?

    A. Principal only (PO) tranches
    B. Planned amortization class (PAC) tranches
    C. Targeted amortization class (TAC) tranches
    D. Interest only (IO) tranches

    i.   A only

    ii.   B only

   iii.   B and C

   iv.   B, C, and D

24.   A client is interested in investing in CMOs for the first time. If safety is her primary concern, which tranches would you recommend?

A. Z

B. TAC

C. Companion

D. PAC

25.   What must you disclose to a customer interested in investing in CMOs for the first time?

A. They are made up of various securities and guaranteed by the US government.

B. All CMOs carry an equal amount of risk.

C. They are triple tax-free investments.

D. They are subject to prepayment and extension risk.

26.   Which two are correct regarding the prepayment of CMOs?

A. When interest rates rise, prepayments increase.

B. Interest rates rise when prepayments decrease.

C. When interest rates fall, prepayments increase.

D. Interest rates fall when prepayments decrease.

    i.   A and C

   ii.   A and D

   iii.   A and C

   iv.   B and D

27.   All of the following are part of a CMO EXCEPT:

A. Government National Mortgage Association, or Ginnie Mae (GNMA)

B. The Federal National Mortgage Association (FNMA)

C. Secondary Loan Market Association (SLMA)

D. Federal Home Loan Mortgage Corporation, or Freddie Mac (FHLMC)

28.   Which two S&P ratings do CMOs typically have?

A. AAA

B. AA

C. A

D. BBB

    i.   A and B

    ii.   B and C

   iii.   C and D

   iv.   B and D

29.   Which are parts of the Farm Credit System (FCS)?

A. Federal Home Loan Banks

B. Federal Intermediate Credit Banks

C. Bank for Cooperatives

D. Federal Land Banks

    i.   A, C, and D

    ii.   A, C, and D

   iii.   A, B, and C

   iv.   A, B, and D

30.   Which is not valid for The Government National Mortgage Association (GNMA)?

A. They issue pass-through certificates.

B. They are backed by commercial, Federal Housing Administration (FHA), and Veterans Affairs (VA) mortgages.

C. They pay interest semiannually.

D. The interest received is subject to federal, state, and local taxes.

31.   Which is TRUE of GNMAs?

A. They are considered safer than FHLMCs.

B. The US government backs them.

C. They pay interest semiannually.

D. The interest received by investors is state-tax-free.

    i.   A and B

    ii.   B, C and D

   iii.   A, C and D

   iv.   A and D

32.   Which agency's securities are a direct obligation of the US government?

    A. FHLMC

    B. GNMA

    C. FNMA

    D. FCS

33.   What are the initial maturities of Treasury bonds?

    A. One month to 1 year

    B. More than 1 year to 10 years

    C. Either 20 or 30 years

    D. Between 1 and 30 years

34.   What is the maximum maturity of a T-note?

    A. One year

    B. Two years

    C. Five years

    D. Ten years

35.   What is the arrangement of the following US government securities in order of initial maturity from shortest to longest term?

    A. Treasury bills

    B. Treasury notes

    C. Treasury bonds

    i.   A, B, and C

    ii.   C, B, and A
    iii.   C, A, and B
    iv.   B, A, and C

36.   Which two are valid concerning T-STRIPS?

    A. Holders do not pay taxes on the interest earned until maturity.
    B. Holders must pay taxes on the interest earned annually.
    C. Holders receive the principal and interest at maturity.
    D. Holders receive interest semiannually, and the principal is paid at maturity.

    i.   A and C
    ii.   A and D
    iii. B and C
    iv. B and D

37.   The following are the benefits of investing in Treasury inflation-protected securities (TIPS) EXCEPT:

    A. A guaranteed profit
    B. They are low-risk investments
    C. The principal keeps pace with inflation
    D. They can be purchased directly through the Treasury Direct system

38.   Which of these Treasury securities earn interest?

    A. Treasury bills
    B. Treasury bonds
    C. Treasury stock
    D. Treasury STRIPS

    i.   B only
    ii.   A, B, and D
    iii. B and C
    iv. C and D

39. All are true for T-bills EXCEPT:

    A. T-bills make semiannual interest payments.
    B. T-bills are issued with 4-, 13-, and 26-week maturities.
    C. Most T-bills are callable.
    D. T-bills are traded on a discount yield basis.

    i.   A and B
    ii. A, B, and C
    iii. B and D
    iv. B, C and D

40. Which security uses the security quote 1.933 – 1.835?

    A. Ginnie Mae
    B. Treasury bill
    C. Treasury note
    D. Treasury bond

41. In what forms does the US government issue Treasury bonds?

    A. Book entry
    B. Bearer
    C. Fully registered
    D. Partially registered

42. A customer has ABC convertible bonds, which convert to 40 ABC common stock. Your customer may convert or call the bonds at 104 when ABC common stock is $28.50. Which situation does your customer face?

    A. A forced conversion
    B. An arbitrage situation
    C. Risk arbitrage
    D. Refunding call

43. A bond is convertible into common stock for $25. If the stock trades at $28, what is the bond's parity price?

A. $990
B. $1,020
C. $1040
D. $1,120

44. The $10 million convertible mortgage bonds from Dyv Corp. are convertible for $40. The bonds mature in March 2030 and are callable in March 2020. Bonds trade at 110, stocks at $48. What is the bond conversion ratio?

A. 10
B. 16.66
C. 20
D. 25

45. A Bond is convertible to 25 common stocks. While the bond trades at 98, stocks are at $40. Which option is best for an investor if the bond is called at 102?

A. Allow the bond to be called.
B. Sell the bond in the market.
C. Convert the bond and sell the stock.
D. None of the above.

46. At $50, Crispy Fry Food Corporation bonds are convertible. Which statement is true if its common stock trades for $42 and bonds at $83?

A. The bonds are trading below parity.
B. The stock is trading below parity.
C. Converting the bonds would be profitable.
D. Converting the bonds would not be profitable.

    i.   A and C
    ii. A and D

      iii.   B and C
      iv.   B and D

47.   TUV convertible bonds are trading at 98. TUV is convertible into common stock at $20. If the common stock is 10% below parity, what is the price of the common stock?

    A. $8.82
    B. $9.80
    C. $17.64
    D. $19.60

48.   Your 65-year-old client started his Roth IRA nine years ago. It is his Roth IRA liquidation and checking account deposit. Which tax implication of this activity is true?

    A. Long-term capital gains tax profits.
    B. Contributions are tax-free, and returns are taxed as long-term gains.
    C. Ordinary income taxes apply to the full distribution.
    D. The full payout is tax-free.

49.   Two brothers are opening a nonqualified account at your office. If one brother dies, they want the assets to go to the other brother. What is the correct account type for this situation?

    A. Partnership
    B. JTWROS
    C. A limited liability company (LLC)
    D. Joint Tenancy in common check

50.   What is a statutory prospectus called?

    A. Red herring
    B. Preliminary prospectus
    C. Final prospectus
    D. Blue-sky prospectus

51.   Former AND Corp. convertible bonds had a $5 million par value. The $25 convertible bonds have an anti-dilution provision. If AND Corp. announces a 5% stock dividend on the ex-dividend date, which of the following is true?

A. The conversion price will increase.
B. The conversion price will decrease.
C. The conversion ratio will increase.
D. The conversion ratio will decrease.

    i.   A and C
   ii.   A and D
  iii.   B and C
   iv.   B and D

52.   An anti-dilution clause is essential to holders of which of the following debt securities?

A. Adjustment bonds
B. Convertible bonds
C. Income bonds
D. Zero-coupon bonds

53.   KR Corporation issued 7% callable bonds. Which case would KR call their bonds in?

A. If interest rates decrease
B. If interest rates remain the same
C. If interest rates increase
D. If interest rates fluctuate

54.   Which is valid for a coupon rate of put bonds vis-a-vis callable bonds, with all else being the same?

A. Lower than
B. The same as
C. Higher than

D. Cannot be determined

55. Which of the following would the issuer most likely refund if a bond's YTM is 5%?

   A. Coupon 5.5%, maturing in 2040, callable in 2031 at 103
   B. Coupon 4.5%, maturing in 2040, callable in 2030 at 103
   C. Coupon 4.5%, maturing in 2040, callable in 2030 at 100
   D. Coupon 5.5%, maturing in 2040, callable in 2031 at 100

   i.   A and B
   ii. B and D
   iii. C only
   iv. D only

56. What is the call premium on a callable bond?

   A. The sum an investor must pay above par value when calling the bonds early
   B. The amount an issuer must pay above par value when calling its bonds early
   C. The sum of interest an issuer must pay on its callable bonds
   D. The difference in interest an issuer must pay on its callable bonds over its non-callable bonds

57. Which of the following BEST describes the call premium for debt securities?

   A. The amount that investors paid above par value to purchase the bond in the primary market
   B. The sum that investors paid above par value to have the bond in the secondary market
   C. The sum that investors must pay to the issuer for having the bond called early
   D. The amount that the issuer must pay to investors for calling its bonds early

58.   Which feature is MOST suitable for an issuer of a corporate bond?

A. A high coupon rate
B. A put feature
C. A high call premium
D. Little call protection

59.   Which is the highest S&P credit rating for high-yield bonds?

A. AAA
B. BBB
C. BB
D. C

60.   Which S&P investment grade credit ratings show the correct arrangement from highest to lowest?

A. A+
B. AA–
C. AA
D. AAA

   i.   D, C, B, A
   ii.   D, A, C, B
   iii. A, D, C, B
   iv.   A, B, C, D

61.   Mrs. L has $10,000. She faces the least capital risk with which investment?

A. Blue chip stocks
B. Investment grade bonds
C. Warrants
D. Call options

62.   Whose signature should be on a new account form?

A. The customer's

B. The broker's

C. A principal's

    i.   A and B

    ii.   A and C

   iii. B and C

   iv. A, B, and C

63.   Which option is correct for a customer who wants to open a new account but refuses to provide some of the requested financial information?

    A. Comprehensive financial details are a must before opening the account.

    B. Open the account and trade unsolicited only.

    C. Confirmation from other sources concerning client affordability is required.

    D. The account can be opened but not traded until the consumer submits financial details.

64.   How often must a firm seek client information about a new account form update?

    A. Annually

    B. Once every two years

    C. Once every three years

    D. Once every four years

65.   Mr S. wants to open an account with a broker-dealer, AMA. He does not want their name visible on the account. How should the broker-dealer handle the request?

    A. AMA would number Mr. S's account.

    B. For accredited investors, AMA would open a street-named account for Mr. S.

    C. AMA won't establish the account till Mr. S consents to their name.

    D. For Mr. S, AMA would use one of its recognized aliases.

66.   What must occur to open a numbered account for a new client?

A. The client must sign a written statement attesting to ownership of the account.
B. The client would need to receive permission from FINRA.
C. The client would need to receive permission from the SEC.
D. Choices b and c.

67.   A client of DEF broker-dealer owns 1,000 shares of ABD Corporation, held in street name. What process will the broker-dealer adopt for a proxy from ABD Corporation?

A. The broker-dealer must forward the proxy to the client.
B. The broker-dealer votes the proxy.
C. The broker-dealer informs ABD Corporation to send the proxy directly to the client.
D. None of the above.

68.   Under the USA Patriot Act, which of these must banks and brokerage firms maintain to help prevent money laundering and the financing of terrorist operations?

A. Customer identification programs (CIPs)
B. Specially Designated Nationals List (SDNs)
C. Office of Foreign Asset Control (OFAC)
D. FinCEN

69.   Which of these must financial institutions maintain as part of the USA Patriot Act of 2001?

A. Customer identification programs
B. A fidelity bond
C. The Securities Investor Protection Corporation (SIPC) coverage
D. All of the above

70. What is the minimum deposit amount of equity for an investor with a day trading account?

    A. $10,000
    B. $15,000
    C. $20,000
    D. $25,000

71. What is the minimum amount of assets for a client to establish a prime brokerage account?

    A. $100,000
    B. $500,000
    C. $1,000,000
    D. $5,000,000

72. Which fee-based accounts charge a single fee for asset allocation, portfolio management, trade execution, and administration?

    A. Wrap accounts
    B. Joint accounts
    C. Day trading accounts
    D. All of the above

73. Mr. and Mrs. F opened a joint account many years back as JTWROS. Mr. F passed away in an accident. Upon receiving confirmation of Mr. F's passing, what should be done with the account?

    A. The joint account transfers to Mrs. F.
    B. The estate would get Mr. F's account.
    C. Distribution is based on investment percentage.
    D. Any of the aforementioned is fine.

74. A husband and wife open a joint account as tenants in common (TIC). If one spouse dies, what should be done with the account?

    A. The survivor gets TIC account.
    B. The deceased's estate receives their account.

C. The account is distributed on investment percentages.

D. None of these.

75. What kind of joint account do unrelated people typically establish with the estate as beneficiary?

A. Joint tenants with rights of survivorship

B. TIC

C. Discretionary account

D. Custodial account

76. If a married individual creates an account in a state with community property laws, what happens to the account when they pass away?

A. It is transferred equally to any children.

B. It is transferred to a spouse.

C. It becomes part of their estate.

D. Any of the above.

77. Each of these individuals may open a joint account EXCEPT?

A. Three friends

B. Two cousins

C. Parent and minor daughter

D. A married couple

78. Which of these are TRUE regarding revocable trusts and irrevocable trusts?

A. Revocable trusts allow beneficiary changes.

B. Revocable trusts cannot alter beneficiaries.

C. An irrevocable trust allows beneficiary changes.

D. Irrevocable trusts cannot alter beneficiaries.

    i.   A and C

    ii.   A and D

   iii. B and C

   iv. B and D

79.   Which period of results must be present in the performance statistics of a ten-year-old mutual fund?

A. Third-year results
B. Fourth-year results
C. Sixth-year results
D. First-year results

80.   Which accounts can a client open without a written power of attorney?

A. Spouse account
B. Account for minor daughter
C. A business partner account
D. None of these

81.   R. wants to create a UGMA account for his 15-year-old daughter as an account custodian. Which is required for UGMA account investments?

A. The legal list
B. The FINRA list of approved investments for minors' accounts
C. The prudent man rule

    i.   A and B
    ii.   A and C
    iii. B and C
    iv.   A, B, and C

82.   Broker-dealers may open a joint account for each of the following couples EXCEPT:

A. A parent and a minor daughter
B. Three unrelated individuals
C. Husband and wife
D. An individual and their 71-year-old mother

83.   What is a UGMA account?

    A. Joint account
    B. Individual account
    C. Custodial account
    D. Trust account

84.   Which is not true about UGMA accounts?

    A. Minors pay taxes.
    B. Minors endorse certificates.
    C. The custodian cannot authorize account power of attorney.
    D. Services of the guardian are unpaid.

85.   Which of these occur under the Uniform Gifts to Minors Act when a minor attains the majority age?

    A. The account changes to UTMA.
    B. The donor gets the account.
    C. Account closed. The broker-dealer pays the ex-minor the market value of the securities in the account.
    D. The ex-minor receives the account.

86.   How should principals approve trades executed in discretionary accounts?

    A. Just before execution
    B. By transaction completion
    C. Before order entry
    D. Immediately after execution

87.   A customer has approved a registered rep limited power of attorney. All are true EXCEPT:

    A. The registered rep cannot remove cash or securities.
    B. Registration allows the salesperson to place unsolicited account orders.
    C. The registered rep needs the principal's permission before executing orders.
    D. A power of attorney immediately expires upon the investor's death.

88. Which two are TRUE regarding a power of attorney?

    A. A durable power of attorney cancels upon mental incompetence or death of the investor.
    B. A durable power of attorney only cancels upon the death of the investor.
    C. A regular power of attorney cancels upon mental incompetence or death of the investor.

        i.   A and C
       ii.   A and D
      iii.   B and C
      iv.   B and D

89. What must the broker-dealer get from a corporate customer who wants to open a cash account for their company?

    A. Corporate charter
    B. Corporate resolution
    C. Corporate charter and corporate resolution
    D. None of the above

90. Which of these is typically used by banks, mutual funds, and insurance companies?

    A. Institutional accounts
    B. Corporate accounts
    C. Partnership accounts
    D. Joint accounts

91. Registered representative Allen works for Nk Securities. Allen just learned that one of their clients died. Allen should do which of these with the dead client's account?

    A. Document the client's account as deceased.
    B. Remove all open orders.
    C. Await for the proper legal papers.

D. All of the above.

92. What should a brokerage firm NOT do if one of their clients dies?

A. Rescind all open orders.
B. Freeze the account.
C. Shift the money in the account to the executor of the estate.
D. Revoke any written power of attorney.

93. Which statement may legally appear in advertisements or sales literature?

A. "Our dedicated sales team is industry-leading."
B. "Our investing advice consistently exceeds the market and will."
C. "We promise each consumer at least 7% annual return on investment."
D. "Our dedicated sales team will help you meet your investment goals."

94. What is the nature of a radio ad created by a broker-dealer to attract new clients?

A. Correspondence
B. Retail communication
C. Institutional communication
D. A violation of FINRA rules

95. A brokerage business may send promotions to how many retail recipients per FINRA rule 2210 for communication purposes?

A. 16
B. 19
C. 25
D. There is no limit.

96. Which accounts require power of attorney?

A. Discretionary accounts
B. Custodial accounts
C. Joint accounts
D. Fiduciary accounts

    i.   A only
    ii.   A and B
    iii. A, B and D
    iv.   A, B, C and D

97. What must a broker-dealer obtain from a corporate customer who wants to open a margin account for their company?

    A. Corporate charter
    B. Corporate resolution
    C. Corporate charter and corporate resolution
    D. None of the above

98. Which age applies to the rules for the financial exploitation of specified adults?

    A. Age 60 and over
    B. Age 65 and over
    C. Age 70 and over
    D. Age 73 and over

99. According to FINRA rules for restraining or addressing cases of monetary exploitation of specified adults, which option pertains to specified adults?

    A. Individuals 65 or older, seniors, or anyone over 70
    B. Individuals 18 or older with mental or physical limitations who cannot safeguard their interests
    C. Individuals 21 or older with mental or physical limitations who cannot safeguard their interests

        i.   A and C
        ii.   A and B
        iii. B and C
        iv.   B only

100. One brokerage company has a senior customer. If it suspects financial exploitation, how long may it hold account distributions?

    A. For 5 business days
    B. For 10 business days
    C. For 15 business days
    D. For 20 business days

101. Which SEC regulation requires brokerage firms to protect non-public consumer data?

    A. Regulation T
    B. Regulation G
    C. Regulation S-P
    D. Regulation A

102. FINRA Rule 4530 requires other member firms to notify which of these about an affiliated firm member?

    A. A customer complaint claiming fraud or securities abuse in writing
    B. Rejected registration, blocked, suspended, or penalized by US or international regulators.
    C. Anyone indicted, convicted, or pleading guilty to a US or foreign crime or misdemeanor.
    D. All the aforementioned

103. A new representative wants to bartend weekends at a local restaurant while writing a book to make income. Which agency must they disclose this information to?

    A. Broker-dealer
    B. Broker-dealer and FINRA
    C. Broker-dealer and the NYSE
    D. Broker-dealer and the Fed

104. What is the procedure for a registered representative to open a new brokerage account at another firm?

    A. Account executives written permission from his firm.
    B. The account executive must ensure his company gets duplicate trade confirmations done in the account.
    C. The account executive needs clearance to trade in the account.

       i.   A only
      ii.   A and B
     iii.   B and C
     iv.   A, B and C

105. What is the correct procedure for a FINRA firm member who wants to open a new account at another brokerage firm?

    A. The new employer must be notified about the account opening.
    B. The employer must get duplicate trade confirmations upon request.
    C. The employer must provide formal approval to open the account.
    D. The employer must authorize account transactions.

       i.   A only
      ii.   A and B
     iii.   A, B and C
     iv.   A, B, C and D

106. A customer orders 100 LMN shares at $45 apiece. The consumer discovered that LMN had dropped significantly before paying for the agreement. They refuse the shares and won't pay. What is the most suitable option?

    A. You will revoke the order.
    B. They must pay for the shares they bought.
    C. You will promptly sell the shares and cover the loss.
    D. Your company will buy securities for inventory.

107. Which information is required on an order ticket?

    A. Registered rep ID

B. A security description
C. Order time
D. Solicited or unsolicited nature of order

    i.   A and B
    ii.   A, B and C
    iii.   A, B and D
    iv.   A, B, C and D

108.   All these are on an order ticket EXCEPT:

A. The name of the brokerage firm
B. The customer's name
C. The quantity of securities
D. The investor's occupation

109.   These are on an order ticket EXCEPT:

A. The customer's signature
B. The registered rep's identification number
C. The number of securities being purchased
D. The customer's account number

110.   Elizabeth wants 1,000 $1.20 Konica Corporation shares. You advise Elizabeth the investment is too risky for her investment profile as her agent. Which option is suitable if she insists on Bic shares?

A. Reject the order.
B. Refuse the order unless Elizabeth alters her investments.
C. Order but label it "unsolicited."
D. Call your principal to try to reason with Elizabeth.

111.   A corporation wants to raise money from non-accredited investors for an IPO. What form of offering permits this money to raise?

A. Regulation D
B. Regulation C
C. Competitive Bid Arrangement

D. Regulation A+

112. Which of these is an example of institutional communication per FINRA?

    A. Billboard advertisements
    B. Magazine advertisements
    C. TV advertisements
    D. Advertisements mailed to banks

113. Antonio is bullish on MIP. He is a long one May 75 call for 8. On expiry day, what is his break-even point?

    A. $67
    B. $83
    C. $120
    D. Insufficient Information

114. Corporation bonds trade at 105. Josephine wants 15 bonds. What is the price of each bond?

    A. $1,050
    B. $1,500
    C. $1,575
    D. $105

115. What is the CY (current yield) of a bond?

    A. Annual interest is divided by par value.
    B. Par value is divided by face value.
    C. Annual interest is divided by market value.
    D. Yield to maturity is divided by par value.

116. What would an analyst examine while analyzing the capital structure of a company?

    A. P/E ratio
    B. Debt to equity ratio

C. Cash ratio

D. Quick ratio

117. MLO stock is trading at $35. A client wrote 30 MNO Corp $20 puts for $5 each. What is the client's maximum gain?

A. $15,000

B. $20,000

C. $32,000

D. He lost

118. All of these solutions have potentially limitless risks EXCEPT:

A. Buying a put debit spread

B. Selling naked calls

C. Shorting 100 shares of ordinary stock

D. Selling a straddle

119. Which facilities are supported by revenue bonds?

A. Highways

B. Middle school, library

C. Toll bridge, power plant

D. A and C only

120. Mrs V desires to purchase AME Corp. stock. The stock was trading at $350. If it pulls back to $320.00, she wants to buy 100 shares. What type of order should she use?

A. Stop

B. Stop-limit

C. Limit

D. All-or-none (AON)

121. All are examples of agency transactions EXCEPT:

A. Broker-dealers find and sell exchange-listed shares to clients.

B. Brokers sell client shares from their inventory.

C. Broker-dealers locate shares to sell to clients using a broker's broker.

D. Broker-dealers offer dark pool shares to clients.

122. What type of security is AHC Corp. stock with 1.26 Beta and 0.29 Alpha? The Russell 2000 Index includes it.

    A. Small tech company
    B. Blue-chip stock
    C. CMO
    D. Regional bank and lender

123. Which measurement describes a stock's volatility compared to the whole market?

    A. Alpha
    B. Gamma
    C. Delta
    D. Beta

124. ASD growth fund has an NAV of $14 and a POP of $15.What is the sales charge percentage?

    A. 7%
    B. 6.6%
    C. 1%
    D. 0.06%

125. Mrs. L is approaching retirement and seeking risk-free investments. She insists on buying a low-cost stock that you believe is too hazardous for her age and financial goals. What should you recommend?

    A. Ignore her request.
    B. Mark the order "unsolicited."
    C. Wait to modify the new account form before accepting the order.
    D. Not accept the order without the principal's permission.

Answer Key

Q.	1	2	3	4	5	6	7	8	9	10	11	12	13	14
A.	C	ii	D	iii	A	B	ii	i	A	D	C	B	A	iv

Q.	15	16	17	18	19	20	21	22	23	24	25	26	27	28
A.	C	D	B	A	C	iv	B	C	C	D	D	iii	C	i

Q.	29	30	31	32	33	34	35	36	37	38	39	40	41	42
A.	i	C	ii	A	C	D	i	iii	A	ii	ii	B	A	A

Q.	43	44	45	46	47	48	49	50	51	52	53	54	55	56
A.	D	D	A	i	C	D	B	C	iii	B	A	A	iv	B

Q.	57	58	59	60	61	62	63	64	65	66	67	68	69	70
A.	D	B	C	i	B	iii	C	C	A	A	A	A	A	D

Q.	71	72	73	74	75	76	77	78	79	80	81	82	83	84
A.	B	A	A	B	B	B	C	ii	D	B	ii	A	C	B

Q.	85	86	87	88	89	90	91	92	93	94	95	96	97	98
A.	D	D	C	iii	B	D	A	C	D	B	C	i	C	B

Q.	99	100	101	102	103	104	105	106	107	108	109	110	111	112
A.	ii	C	C	D	A	ii	iii	B	iv	D	A	C	D	D

Q.	113	114	115	116	117	118	119	120	121	122	123	124	125
A.	B	A	C	B	A	A	D	C	B	A	D	B	B

Answer Key and Explanations

1. C. It is a private placement and cannot be offered to more than 35 unaccredited investors annually.

2. ii. Any representation that the SEC or self-regulatory body authorized or guaranteed an issue is false. The SEC clarifies. It reviews registration statements and provides cooling-off stop orders.

3. D. Marketing the new security and soliciting sales during the cooling-off period is illegal.

4. iii. Companies selling securities must register with the SEC and issue a prospectus. The syndicate manager handles tombstone advertisements, not the issuer.

5. A. Newspapers print tombstone advertising. Companies announce new securities issuance with tombstone ads. The ad specifies the issuer, syndicate manager, and members but not the sellers.

6. B. Switching dividends and capital gains to cash may boost Isabel's earnings. She rejects back-end load sales charges for Class B Mutual Funds, and her weak assets make municipal bonds unattractive.

7. ii. Interest in a new item doesn't bind consumers or brokers. Consumers may claim they want all Zzow shares when they become available and then change their minds. Even if the customer showed interest in Zzow, the broker-dealer doesn't have to sell all available shares.

8. i. Issuers may register securities in states by filing, coordinating, or qualifying.

9. A. Notification is the easiest way to register existing firms. Previous issuers in a state may renew their application.

10. D. Qualification. Registration by qualification is state mandated if an offering is not registered under the Securities Act.

11. C. The syndicate manager determines the public offering price, takedown, and order allocation. The SEC defines the effective date (the first trading day).

12. B. A statement that the SEC sanctions or guarantees an issuer, issue, or broker-dealer is false. The SEC clears an effective issue.

13. A. The Securities Act (1933) covers the sale of new issues (primary market). It provides more transparency in financial statements and curbs issuers' fraudulent activities.

14. iv. The Securities and Exchange Act includes margin account rules, the issuing of proxies, short sale rules, etC. The Trust Indenture Act covers trust indentures (1939).

15. C. Under the Trust Indenture Act, Investors must get an indenture for corporate bonds valued above $50 million.

16. D. Investment banks provide various services to issuers and high-networth customers. They help new issuers raise money, comply with securities rules, and sell securities.

17. B. The Federal Reserve Board (FRB) discount rate sets the interest rate. Eurodollar deposits, kept in foreign institutions, carry more risk and interest; the rate is unrelated to the Federal Reserve Board.

18. A. Money market instruments are typically one year or less and are short-term debt securities.

19. C. Small investors shouldn't buy negotiable CDs. Trading starts at $100,000, generally in $1 million pieces. Only institutional investors purchase and sell negotiable CDs due to the high minimum denomination.

20. iv. CDOs are asset-backed like credit cards and auto loans. They are not suitable for everyone.

21. B. Credit cards, auto loans, and rarely mortgages secure CDOs.

22.   C. Collateralized mortgage obligations (CMOs) are unique investments and can only be compared to other CMOs.

23.   C. Companion tranches absorb the prepayment risk associated with CMOs. A companion tranche backs all PAC and TAC tranches.

24.   D. The planned amortization class (PAC) tranche is safest. TAC is riskier than PAC. Investors aren't paid until all CMO tranches are retired, making Z-tranches the most volatile.

25.   D. CMOs face prepayment and extension risks linked to current mortgage interest rates. CMOs are taxed at all levels.

26.   iii. Mortgage interest rates strongly influence CMO maturity. Prepayments will rise as more homeowners refinance to take advantage of interest rates when reduceD. If loan rates increase, homeowners won't refinance, reducing prepayments.

27.   C. Sallie Mae (SLMA) is an agency that issues bonds to fund student loans and is not a part of a CMO.

28.   i. CMOs usually receive a AAA or AA S&P rating due to their US government and federal agency mortgage backing.

29.   i. The question keyword is "farm." Bank for Cooperatives (COOPs), Federal Land Banks (FLBs), and Federal Intermediate Credit Banks (FICB) constitute the Federal Farm Credit System. These institutions lend to farmers, not homeowners.

30.   C. Unlike most debt instruments, Ginnie Maes (GNMAs) pay interest monthly like mortgages, not semiannually.

31.   ii. GNMAs are the only agency securities supported by the complete trust and credit of the US government.

32.   A. Ginnie Maes are considered safer investments than Freddie Macs. GNMAs pay monthly interest and are taxed on all levels (federal, state,

and local). GNMAs are issued with a face value of $25,000 but can be bought in denominations as low as $1,000.

33.   C. Treasury bonds (T-bonds) have the longest maturity. Their initial maturity is 20 or 30 years.

34.   D. Treasury securities have the following maximum maturities:

   a.   T-bills: 1-year
   b.   T-notes: 10 years
   c.   T-bonds: 30 years
   d.   T-STRIPS: 30 years

35.   i. Treasury bills have maturities of 4, 8, 13, 26, and 52 weeks. Treasury notes have maturities of 2, 3, 5, 7, and 10 years. Treasury bonds have maturities of 20 or 30 years.

36.   iii. Treasury STRIPS (T-STRIPS) are bought at a discount and mature at par value. The principal and interest are received only at maturity.

37.   A. TIPS are marketable 5-, 10-, and 30-year US government securities. They pay semiannual principal-based interest. Due to the bond's Consumer Price Index (CPI)-linked principal, interest payments may rise or fall with inflation or deflation. At maturity, holders get the face value or adjusted principal. Investors may lose money if they sell low-risk assets for less than their cost basis.

38.   ii. The keyword is "earn." STRIPS and Treasury note holders earn interest without receiving it. Interest is due on discounted Treasury notes and Treasury STRIPS maturing at par. Treasury bondholders earn biannual interest. Corporations issue and repurchase Treasury stock. Stockholders never receive interest but get occasional dividends.

39.   ii. T-bills are short-term and uncallable. They're sold at a discount yield because they're listed in yields, not prices.

40. B. The bid and ask prices are usually lower on the left. This time, the left number is larger. T-bill quotes have this functionality. Discount yield T-bills have a greater bid than ask. If yields were converted to prices, the left number would be lower than the right, like other securities.

41. A. Since the mid-1980s, the US government issued book-entry securities. Trading book-entry securities requires no certificate. A central agency maintains ownership data, and investors get a security receipt.

42. A. The bond is being called at $1,040 (104% of $1,000 par) or is convertible into common stock valuing $1,140 ($28.50 × 40). The investors would lose $100 ($1140 – $1040) by accepting the call and not converting. Situations like this are dubbed forced conversions. Corporations may also issue reverse convertible bonds to convert the bonds at a predetermined date.

43. D. Consider the shares with convertible bond questions. To determine how many shares the bond is convertible into, use the formula: Conversion ratio = Par / Conversion price, or 1000/25 = 40 shares. To calculate the parity price of the stock, multiply the number of shares by the stock's market price: 40×28 = $1,120

44. D. The conversion ratio is the number of shares a convertible bond (or stock) is converted into. Use the following formula to calculate:

Conversion ratio = Par / Conversion price

1000/40 = 25

The par value for the bonds is assumed to be $1,000. If an investor converted one of their bonds, they would receive 25 shares of the company's common stock.

45. A. Consider the amount of money the investor is receiving for the call, selling the bond in the market, or converting it. Whichever is highest is best for the investor.

For allowing the bond to be called: $1,020 (102% of $1,000 par)

For vending the bond in the market: $980 (98% of $1,000 par)

Converting the bond and vending the stock: $1,000 (25× 40)

The best is to call the bond because the investor will receive $1,020, more than the other two choices.

46.   i. To determine the stock's parity price, multiply the market price by the number of shares: Par / Conversion price or 1000/25 = 20 shares. The bond is trading for $830 (83% of $1,000 par) and is convertible into $840 worth of stock. The bonds are trading below parity, and converting them would be advantageous.

47.   C. When dealing with convertible bond questions, determine the amount of shares the bond is convertible into. The bond is convertible at $20: Par / Conversion price or 1000/20 = 50 shares. To determine the parity price, divide the market price (98% of $1,000 par, or $980) of the bond by the conversion ratio: 980/50 = $19.60. If the stock's parity price is $19.60, its value is $17.64 ($19.60 – $1.96), 10% below parity.

48.   D. Roth IRA withdrawals are tax-free for customers aged 59 ½ or older with an open account for at least five years. It includes revenues and donations. Roth IRA contributions are after-tax.

49.   B. A joint tenancy with rights of survivorship (JTWROS) account is suitable since the dead joint tenant's assets flow to the surviving joint tenant.

50.   C. A statutory prospectus is a final prospectus.

51.   iii. A stock dividend gives investors additional shares at a cheaper price. Due to stock dividends, the company lowers the market price and conversion price. As the conversion price falls, the bond's conversion ratio rises.

52.   B. An anti-dilution clause is essential to holders of convertible bonds to safeguard conversion rights.

53.   A. Lower interest rates make issuers more inclined to call bonds. Calling their bonds and issuing new ones with a lower interest rate might save them money.

54.   A. Puttable bonds benefit investors. Investors may "put" bonds back to the issuer at any time at the price listed in the indenture. They provide investors with greater choice and a lower coupon rate.

55.   iv. From the issuer's perspective, they will likely refund the issue that will cost them the most over time. An issuer starts with the coupon rate (highest coupon first), then call premium (lowest call premium first), call date (earliest call date first), and then maturity.

56.   B. A call premium is a sum over the par value an issuer pays if it calls its bonds earlier.

57.   D. Issuers pay call premiums to investors for early bond calls. To discourage early bond calls, a firm pays a call premium above par value.

58.   B. Corporations dislike high coupon rates, put features, and call premiums. Some call protection on callable bonds is beneficial. Call protection is how long an issuer must wait to call bonds.

59.   C. S&P ratings of BB and lower are considered high-yield (speculative or junk) bonds. The default risk is higher for lower ratings.

60.   i. The AA ratings, from highest to lowest, are AA+, AA, and AA−. Of the given options, from highest to lowest, the ranks are AAA, AA, AA-, and A+. Yield is higher for lower ratings (more risk = more reward).

61.   B. Investment-grade bonds are the safest choice. Investment grade bondholders get par value at maturity regardless of market performance.

62.   iii. Clients may not sign new accounts. The broker must fill out and sign the new account form and have the principal sign it.

63.   C. Using other sources, the licensed broker makes recommendations and trades for the customer without complete financial information. Otherwise, brokers can only recommend mutual funds and US government securities for all investors.

64.   C. Firms must update customer information at least once every three years.

65.   A. Broker-dealers usually have street-named or numbered accounts. Numbers or codes are on all order tickets. The broke-dealer must have a signed document stating Mr. S is the account owner.

66.   A. Numbered or street-named accounts require clients' signed paperwork. Accounts of different investors cannot be commingled. The firm must keep this client's account segregated from his other accounts held in the street name.

67.   A. The broker-dealer must forward the proxy to the client after receiving it from the firm.

68.   A. To combat money laundering and terrorism funding, broker-dealers and banks must retain client CIPs under the US Patriot Act.

69.   A. Firms must obtain CIP containing the client's social security number. Other features include date of birth, name, and address, without P.O. boxes.

70.   D. The minimum deposit amount to open a day trading account is $25,000.

71.   B. At least $500,000 worth of assets must be available to establish a prime brokerage account.

72.   A. Wrap accounts include charges for advisory fees, commissions, and other client services by an adviser.

73.   A. For JTWROS, the entire account is transferred to Mrs. F.

74. B. A joint account with a TIC provision transfers the deceased's part to their estate. The survivors inherit the whole account with survivorship rights.

75. B. A joint account with a TIC provision transfers the deceased's half to their estate and the rest to survivors' accounts based on ownership parity.

76. B. Community property accounts resemble JTWROS. Only married couples may use them. Some states mandate transferring the account to the remaining spouse when one spouse dies.

77. C. A joint account is in the name of more than one adult. An account for a minor must be a custodial account.

78. ii. A trustee can revoke or change a revocable trust.

79. D. The first-year result is the most significant.

80. B. Anyone may open and trade the minor's account without a written power of attorney (POA).

81. ii. Fiduciary accounts like UGMA and UTMA must follow the prudent man rule/legal list for the state where the account is set.

82. A. A joint account only has the names of adults.

83. C. Custodial accounts are "managed accounts" for the minor's benefit. An UGMA account has only one custodian and one minor.

84. B. The custodian endorses all certificates for a UGMA account.

85. D. Depending on the state, the account must be handed to the former minor when they reach the age of majority (18-21).

86. D. Principals must authorize discretionary or non-discretionary deals directly after execution. FINRA says permission before execution may delay and undercut prices.

87. C. A limited power of attorney doesn't require permission for each trade execution.

88. iii. A durable power of attorney cancels upon the death of the client. A regular authorization can also be canceled with the client's mental incapacitation.

89. B. A corporate resolution that designates who has trading authority for the account would be required.

90. D. Institutional accounts include mutual funds, banks, insurance firms, etc.

91. A. Document the client's account as deceased.

92. C. Following the death of a client, all open orders must be canceled, the account frozen, and written power of attorney canceled until obtaining instructions from the estate executor.

93. D. While corporations cannot guarantee the other promises, they may say their sales force will help investors achieve their goals.

94. B. Television, radio, magazine, and newspaper ads are retail communications. Retail communication includes written or electronic communication to not more than 25 retail investors in a 30-day period.

95. C. Correspondence resembles retail communication but is sent to 25 or fewer retail investors within any 30-day calendar period.

96. i. Discretionary accounts require power of attorney or trading authorization at the time of execution.

97. C. A corporate charter states the corporation is allowed to purchase on margin and a corporate resolution states who is authorized to trade.

98. B. The financial exploitation rules for specified adults are for seniors or natural persons 65 years of age and over.

99.   ii. Financial exploitation rules of specified adults are for seniors, or natural persons 65 years and over, and natural persons 18 years or older with physical or mental impairments that disable them to safeguard their interests.

100.   C. A hold on withdrawals can be for up to 15 business days.

101.   C. Regulation S-P per The Gramm-Leach-Bliley Act provides safeguards to protect client records from unsolicited uses, including divulging social security numbers, account balances, transaction records, etc.

102.   D. All these are reportable offenses.

103.   A. Moonlighting rules for registered reps mandate that they disclose job information outside the employing firm only to their hiring brokerage firm.

104.   ii. If an employee of a brokerage firm (or their immediate family) opens a new account at another brokerage firm, they must get written permission from the employing firm, sometimes in duplicate.

105.   iii. The agent must write about an account opening to the firm because they work for a FINRA firm. Once the account is opened, they don't need permission to trade.

106.   B. Immediately following a purchase order, a client owns the securities and must pay for them regardless of what happens to the market price.

107.   iv. Registered reps should provide their ID, securities descriptions, order time, and solicitation status on order tickets.

108.   D. The investor's profession is on a new account form, not an order ticket.

109.   A. Most clients would order on the phone, making signature redundant for an order ticket.

110.   C. Marking it as unsolicited protects the registered rep. However, you cannot accept two unsolicited orders: options (unless approved accounts) and direct participation programs (DPPs).

111.   D. The JOBS Act amended Regulation A+ (previously Regulation A). Non-accredited investors may invest in Reg A+ offerings.

112.   D. Institutional communication is any communication made to institutional entities or individuals with at least $50 million in assets.

113.   B. The trade requires the stock to beat or over $83 (75 + $8 = $83) on expiry day for Antonio to break even.

114.   A. Corporate bond quotes are a percentage of $1,000. 105% of $1000 = $1,050.00.

115.   C. CY = Annual interest / Market value

116.   B. The debt-to-equity ratio compares the company's liabilities to the shareholders' equity.

117.   A. Option writers (sellers) have a maximum gain potential based on the premium received. The amount received is $500 for each put: 30 x $500 = $15,000.

118.   A. An options spread (call "spread" or "put spread") limits investor risk to the spread price. Three tactics have potentially limitless risks.

119.   D. Revenue bonds finance income-generating highways, toll roads, and power plants.

120.   C. A limit order specifies an order.

121.   B. A principal transaction occurs when a broker-dealer sells shares from its inventory. Agency transactions occur when broker-dealers find shares elsewhere.

122.   A. A high beta and inclusion into the Russell 2000 Index make AHC a probable small tech firm.

123.   D. Beta describes a stock's volatility.

124. B. Sales charge% = (POP-NAV) / POP or, 6.6%

125. B. Take the order, marking it as unsolicited. It puts liability on the client.

Chapter Seven: Practice Test II

You have three hours to complete the 125 questions in this test.

1.   Whose signature must be present on all order tickets?

    A. A principal
    B. The customer
    C. The state administrator
    D. A compliance officer

2.   When should principals approve trades made by registered representatives?

    A. At or before execution
    B. At or before the completion of the transaction
    C. The same day as the execution of the order
    D. None of the above

3.   How long does a corporate bond take to settle?

    A. One business day
    B. Four business days
    C. Two business days
    D. Five business days

4.   When is payment received for corporate bonds?

A. Within 7 business days
B. Within 3 business days
C. Within 4 business days
D. Within 6 business days

5.   A customer buys 1,000 shares of ABC common stock on Friday, October 3. What is the payment date?

A. Monday, October 6
B. Tuesday, October 7
C. Wednesday, October 8
D. Thursday, October 9

6.   How long does municipal bonds take to settle?

A. One business day after the trade date
B. Five business days after the trade date
C. Two business days after the trade date
D. Four business days after the trade date

7.   When is the payment due for munis after the trade date?

A. Three business days after the trade date
B. Two business days after the trade date
C. Four business days after the trade date
D. Five business days after the trade date

8.   What is the settlement date for US government bond transactions?

A. One business day after the trade date
B. Two business days after the trade date
C. Three business days after the trade date
D. The same day as the trade date

9.   How many business days (s) after the trade date does an options trade settle?

   A. One
   B. Two
   C. Three
   D. Four

10.   Melinda bought 100 TKR common stock for $33 on Friday, October 9. When does this trade settle?

   A. Friday, October 9, on a cash basis or Wednesday, October 14 regular way
   B. Friday, October 9, on a cash basis or Tuesday, October 13 regular way
   C. Monday, October 12, on a cash basis or Tuesday, October 13 regular way
   D. Monday, October 12, on a cash basis or Wednesday, October 14 regular way

11.   The two broker-dealers exchange securities, but one thinks they traded a different number of shares. Which of these must at least one broker-dealer submit?

   A. Don't know (DK)
   B. Rejection letter
   C. Due bill
   D. None of the above

12.   Which of these organizations can grant an extension for the payment of a trade?

   A. The New York Stock Exchange
   B. The Pacific Stock Exchange
   C. FINRA
   D. All of the above

13. Clients with cash accounts buy stock. The client calls five business days later to indicate they cannot pay for the product. How would the broker-dealer act?

    A. Send an application to FINRA to get an extension.
    B. Give the client a two-day extension.
    C. Sell out the stock and freeze the account for 90 days.
    D. Sell out the stock and if there are no losses, there is no penalty.

14. Their account was locked when M. Smith failed to pay for a deal. What does Smith need to do to buy more account securities?

    A. Before executing the purchase order, they must deposit the entire security price.
    B. They must get the principal's permission.
    C. They must wait for the account to unfreeze.
    D. They must deposit the entire security purchase amount before settlement.

15. What certificate with all the trade details is sent out to customers after the trade?

    A. Proxy
    B. Order ticket
    C. Confirmation
    D. Account statement

16. A brokerage firm sent a client confirmation about their latest TRD Corp. common stock trade. Which item should be on this confirmation note?

    A. The trade date and the settlement date
    B. Whether the broker-dealer acted as an agent or principal
    C. The name of the security and how many shares were traded
    D. The amount of commission paid if the broker-dealer acted as an agent

        i.   A and C
        ii.   A, B, and C

  iii. A, C and D
  iv. A, B, C and D

17. When should a member firm send a trade confirmation for member-to-customer transactions?

 A. At or prior to the completion of the transaction
 B. No later than one business day after the trade date
 C. No later than two business days after the trade date
 D. No later than three business days after the trade date

18. Which of the following should be included in a client's confirmation concerning a principal transaction?

 A. The markup and markdown
 B. Registered rep's ID
 C. The commission for an agency transaction
 D. A description of the security

  i. A and C
  ii. A, B and C
  iii. B, C and D
  iv. A, B, C and D

19. Which is essential for the client's confirmation under Municipal Securities Rulemaking Board (MSRB) rules?

 A. The markup or markdown
 B. The location of the bond resolution
 C. The settlement date
 D. Whether the trade was executed on a dealer or agency basis

20. Which of the following is NOT on an order ticket?

 A. Whether the trade was solicited or unsolicited
 B. The amount of commission charged on a broker transaction
 C. The trade date
 D. The address of the brokerage firm delivering the confirmation

21. According to SEC Rule 10b-10, confirmations of trades executed between firms must be sent by which date?

    A. The trade date
    B. One business day following the trade date
    C. The completion of the transaction
    D. Three business days following the trade date

22. Who may not validate a mutilated certificate?

    A. Issuer
    B. Broker-dealer
    C. Registrar
    D. Transfer agent

23. All can be reasons to reject a delivery of municipal bond certificates EXCEPT:

    A. The indenture is illegible
    B. A change in the market price
    C. A missing legal opinion
    D. A misspelling of the investor's name

24. For a trade of 670 shares, all are good deliveries EXCEPT:

    A. Four certificates for 150 shares each and 14 certificates for 5 shares each
    B. One certificate for 600 shares each and 7 certificates for 10 shares each
    C. Three hundred certificates for 2 shares each
    D. Two certificates for 300 shares each and 70 certificates for 1 share each

25. What is returning previously accepted securities called?

    A. Reclamation
    B. Buy-in
    C. Sell-out
    D. Rejection

26.   When does the rejection of securities happen?

A. At the time of delivery
B. Before transactions
C. After transactions
D. None of the above

27.   How can a client holding 200 shares of stock acquire protection?

A. Purchasing another 100 shares of the stock
B. Purchasing an automobile
C. Purchasing a put
D. Trading a put

28.   To generate an opinion on a new municipal bond issue, the bond counsel will review all of the following EXCEPT:

A. Municipal statutes
B. State constitution and amendments
C. Tax code and interpretive regulations
D. Securities Act of 1933

29.   What is the buy-in date if a customer offers securities but fails to deliver?

A. One business day after the trade date
B. Three business days after the trade date
C. Five business days after the trade date
D. Ten business days after the settlement date

30.   In which of the following instances would the seller send the stock buyer a due bill to prove ownership for dividends?

A. The trade is executed before the ex-dividend date.
B. The trade is executed after the ex-dividend date.
C. The trade settles before the record date.
D. The trade settles after the record date.

    i.   A and C

        ii.   A and D
       iii.   B and C
       iv.   B and D

31. How can investors keep stock or bond certificates in book entry form instead of getting them physically?

    A. Direct registration system (DRS)
    B. Securities Investor Protection Corporation (SIPC)
    C. National Adjudicatory Council (NAC)
    D. Delivery versus payment (DVP)

32. All are the responsibilities of the transfer agent EXCEPT:

    A. Good delivery of certificates
    B. Making sure that issued shares do not exceed authorized shares
    C. Delivering proxies to investors
    D. Canceling old certificates for each trade

33. How often must an active account holder who trades multiple times a month get account statements?

    A. Monthly
    B. Quarterly
    C. Semiannually
    D. Annually

34. At what intervals must a brokerage firm client receive an account statement?

    A. Monthly
    B. Two monthly
    C. Quarterly
    D. Yearly

35. What is the time interval for mutual funds to send out account statements to investors?

    A. Monthly
    B. Quarterly
    C. Semiannually
    D. Annually

36. Which set is true for clients regarding receiving account statements per FINRA and SEC standards?

    A. Monthly for active accounts
    B. Quarterly for active accounts
    C. Quarterly for mutual funds
    D. Semiannually for mutual funds

        i.   A and C
        ii. A and D
        iii. B and C
        iv. B and D

37. If a business declares a dividend payable to shareholders of record on Thursday, September 17, what is the ex-dividend date?

    A. Monday, September 14
    B. Tuesday, September 15
    C. Wednesday, September 16
    D. Monday, September 21

38. What is the ex-dividend date?

    A. One business day before the record date
    B. Three business days before the record date
    C. One business day before the payment date
    D. Two business days before the payment date

39. Arrange the following in first-to-last order:

    A. Record date
    B. Ex-dividend date
    C. Payment date
    D. Declaration date

        i.   A, B, C, and D
       ii.   B, C, A, and D
      iii.   D, A, B, and C
      iv.   D, B, A, and C

40. ABN Corporation declares a dividend with a record date of Wednesday, October 17. When is your client's last date to buy the stock the "regular way" and still receive dividends?

    A. Monday, October 15
    B. Tuesday, October 16
    C. Wednesday, October 17
    D. Monday, October 22

41. A business declares a dividend with a record date of Thursday, August 15. If an investor wants to sell the stock and receive the dividend, at which date should the investor sell the stock?

    A. Tuesday, August 13
    B. Wednesday, August 14
    C. Thursday, August 15, on a cash basis
    D. Friday, August 16, on a cash basis

        i.   A and C
       ii.   A and D
      iii.   B and C
      iv.   B and D

42.   Mr. Simmons submitted a complaint letter regarding their recent purchase of blue chip stocks to their broker-dealer. What must a broker-dealer do upon the receipt of the complaint?

A. Return the commission charged.
B. Accept the complaint and write down any action taken.
C. Guarantee to show him the profit.
D. Repurchase the stocks at a price that is at or slightly above Mr. Simmon's purchase price.

43.   In disputes handled through the Code of Procedure (COP), which of the following is TRUE?

A. The consumer chose COP, and court decisions are appealable.
B. The buyer chose COP, and court decisions are non-appealable.
C. The brokerage business chose COP, and court decisions are appealable.
D. The brokerage business chose COP, and court decisions are non-appealable.

44.   Which option is TRUE regarding arbitration decisions?

A. Decisions are binding and non-appealable.
B. Decisions that are not binding are appealable.
C. Members may take non-members to arbitration.
D. Non-members may take members to arbitration.

    i.   A and C
   ii.   A and D
  iii.   B and C
  iv.   B and D

45.   All are TRUE about arbitration EXCEPT:

A. Members may take non-members to arbitration.
B. Non-members may take members to arbitration.
C. Members may take other members to arbitration.
D. Decisions are binding and non-appealable.

46. What is the value of simplified arbitration used for member-to-member disputes?

   A. Not over $10,000
   B. Over $25,000
   C. Not over $50,000
   D. Over $100,000

47. How long does a member have to adhere to the terms of the arbitration decision in the event of a loss?

   A. For 15 days
   B. For 30 days
   C. For 45 days
   D. For 60 days

48. Regarding arbitration and mediation, which TWO of the following are TRUE?

   A. Arbitration decisions are binding and cannot be appealed.
   B. Arbitration decisions are not binding and can be appealed.
   C. Mediation decisions are binding and cannot be appealed.
   D. Mediation decisions are not binding and can be appealed.

      i.   A and C
      ii. A and D
      iii. B and C
      iv. B and D

49. Which affiliation does a brokerage firm need to process an Automated Customer Account Transfer (ACAT)?

   A. FINRA
   B. National Securities Clearing Corporation (NSCC)
   C. Direct Registration System (DRS)
   D. Securities Investor Protection Corporation (SIPC)

50. According to FINRA rules, which is true about ACATs?

A. Firms have one working day to check client instructions after receiving ACAT warnings.
B. Firms have three working days to verify client instructions after receiving ACAT warnings.
C. Transfer assets within three business days after verification.
D. Transfer assets within four business days after verification.

    i.   a and c
    ii.   a and d
    iii.   b and c
    iv.   b and d

51. Per MSRB Rule G-39, which of the following is TRUE of cold-calling?

A. Call the customers after 8:00 am and before 9:00 pm local time.
B. Call customers after 9:00 am and before 8:00 pm local time.
C. After 8:00 am and before 9:00 pm local time, callers must call.
D. Callers must call after 9:00 am and before 8:00 pm local time.

52. Mr. S requested to be placed on your firm's do-not-call list. How long must your firm members wait before contacting Mr. Silva again?

A. One year
B. Two years
C. Five years
D. Life

53. Which factors may NOT be used in determining the markup charged to customers?

A. The market price of the security sold
B. The price the dealer paid to purchase the security
C. Trading size
D. Trading expenses

54. Which of the following applies to the 5% markup policy?

    A. IPOs
    B. The sale of mutual fund shares
    C. Regulation D offerings
    D. The over-the-counter sale of outstanding non-exempt securities

55. Which of the following types of secondary market transactions APPLY the 5% markup policy?

    A. Riskless or simultaneous transactions
    B. Common stock sold from a dealer's inventory
    C. Proceeds transactions on non-exempt securities
    D. All of the above

56. What is the formula for equity for a Short Margin Account?

    A. Equity = (+ Credit - Short Market Value)
    B. Equity = (+ Credit + Short Market Value)
    C. Equity = (- Credit + Short Market Value)
    D. Equity = (- Credit - Short Market Value)

57. All are valid about municipal financial advisors in competitive bid underwritings EXCEPT:

    A. The issuer pays the financial advisor.
    B. The financial advisor is the underwriter of the offering.
    C. A financial advisor is generally a municipal broker-dealer.
    D. A financial advisor enables the issuer to set a new bond offering.

58. For options trading, which is "advertisement" per the Securities Act of 1933?

    A. Options disclosure document
    B. Options website
    C. Personal letters sent to customers
    D. Standard option worksheet

59.   What is quantitative easing (QI)?

A. Decreasing interest rates
B. Raising interest rates
C. Measurement of security volatility
D. The Central bank sells securities to lower the money supply

60.   What is the principal role of the Federal Reserve?

A. Regulate stock exchange
B. Enforce tax laws
C. Control interest rates
D. Manage foreign trades

61.   Which is true for a convertible bond?

A. It can be converted into the issuing firm's stock.
B. The issuer can repurchase it.
C. It pays fixed interest rates.
D. A foreign business issues a bond.

62.   What is a margin call?

A. Requests more collateral on a margin account
B. Informs stock splits
C. Offers new investment options
D. Requests for early retirement

63.   What is a 401 (k)?

A. Kind of bond
B. Retirement savings plan
C. Kind of stock
D. Tax form

64. What is the full form for an IPO?

   A. Internal Product Option
   B. Initial Public Offering
   C. Investment Profit Offering
   D. Initial Price Option

65. What is a stop-loss order?

   A. Purchasing stocks at a specific price
   B. Selling stocks at a certain price
   C. Stopping all trading activities
   D. Purchasing more stocks at market value

66. What is an option?

   A. A type of bond
   B. Right to trade an asset at an agreed price under specified conditions
   C. A mutual fund
   D. Fixed interest rates

67. What is a primary market?

   A. A place to buy securities directly from the firms
   B. A place to exchange securities
   C. Type of commodities market
   D. A Market for derivatives

68. What is the feature of a closed-end fund?

   A. Not available to new investors
   B. A fixed share number
   C. Index tracking
   D. Start-up investment

69. What is EBITDA?

    A. Earnings Before Interest, Taxes, Depreciation, and Amortization
    B. Earnings Before Investment, Trade, Dividend, and Asset
    C. Earnings by Internal Tax Department Assessment
    D. Estimated Business Income, Tax, Duties, and Assessment

70. Which of these descriptions fit a hedge fund?

    A. A mutual fund
    B. Strategy to earn active interest
    C. Agricultural commodities investment
    D. Retirement fund

71. What is the P/E ratio?

    A. Profits to Earnings ratio
    B. Price to Earnings ratio
    C. Profit to Profit
    D. Price to Equity ratio

72. What makes insider trading illegal?

    A. Public information-based trading
    B. Confidential information
    C. Simultaneous selling of large share amounts
    D. Simultaneous buying of large share amounts

73. Which of these fits a junk bond description?

    A. Default
    B. High-interest rate
    C. Below investment grade
    D. Start-up

74.   What is short selling?

A. Selling current shares
B. purchasing shares with a loan
C. Selling borrowed shares intending to repurchase them at a lower price
D. Purchasing and selling shares on the same day

75.   What is day trading?

A. Multiple trading of shares on the same day
B. Holding shares for over a year
C. Trading on Mondays only
D. Holding shares for less than a month

76.   What is an annuity?

A. A lump-sum amount
B. Regular dividends
C. Life insurance
D. Loan

77.   What is an ROI?

A. Roll Over Investments
B. Rate of Interest
C. Return on Investment
D. Rate of Inflation

78.   What is an illiquid asset?

A. It is easy to procure and sell
B. It gives high returns
C. It is prone to default
D. It is difficult to procure and sell

79.   Which of these fits a bid price description?

A. The investor is willing to sell at this price
B. The security's best price on a trading day
C. The price at which the investor is willing to purchase
D. The security's lowest price on a trading day

80.   Which one is a blue chip stock?

A. Start-up stocks
B. Large company stocks
C. Stable company stocks
D. Stocks paying high dividends

81.   What is a put?

A. The right to stock purchases at a specified price before a given date.
B. It increases in value with a rising stock price.
C. It expires when the stock price falls.
D. The right to stock trading at a specified price before a given date.

82.   What is market capitalization?

A. Total dollar market value of the firm's shares
B. Total firm assets
C. The capital raised via IPO
D. Total company liabilities

83.   What is the coupon rate?

A. Fluctuation rate of bond prices
B. Interest on bond
C. Rate of bond conversion to stock
D. Rate of bond maturity

84. What is a preferred stock?

    A. Stock with voting rights
    B. Stock with fixed dividends
    C. Stocks without voting rights
    D. Stocks for institutional investors

85. What is an index?

    A. A benchmark
    B. Mutual fund
    C. Bond
    D. A trading platform

86. Which is an alpha?

    A. Average return
    B. Excess investment returns
    C. Investment-associated risks
    D. Stock yield measurement

87. What describes a growth stock?

    A. High dividend
    B. History of stable growth
    C. Above-average growth rate
    D. High P/E ratio

88. What best describes a day trader?

    A. A long-time trader
    B. One who trades securities within the same day
    C. One who trades options only
    D. One who trades once per week

89. Which of these is unethical trading?

   A. Public information-based trading
   B. Trading on inside information
   C. Trading by day traders
   D. Trading based on analyst recommendations

90. What is leverage?

   A. Borrowed money usage to raise returns
   B. Short selling securities
   C. Trading cost of securities
   D. Portfolio percentage of stocks

91. What is a limit order?

   A. An order to trade at a precise price or better
   B. An order to trade at the current market value
   C. The order turns into a market order after a specific price
   D. The order is valid only for the day

92. What is the main objective of an IPO?

   A. Enabling the issuer to repurchase securities
   B. Allowing the firm to go public and raise capital
   C. Enabling the firm to liquidate its assets
   D. Enabling the firm to pay dividends

93. What is a bid-ask spread?

   A. Difference between the maximum price a buyer is willing to pay and
      the lowest offered by the bidder
   B. Auction price ranges
   C. Option contract's cost
   D. Opening price less by the closing price

94.   What is dollar-cost averaging?

    A. Investing a fixed dollar amount regularly
    B. Investing only in a down-trending market
    C. Purchasing securities in $200 increments
    D. Selling dollar-appreciated stocks

95.   What is the margin call for an investor buying 100 shares at $20/share in an initial transaction on a margin account?

    A. $1,800
    B. $980
    C. $2,000
    D. $20,000

96.   What is a zero-coupon bond?

    A. A no-interest bond
    B. Maturity payments only
    C. Annual payments
    D. Monthly dividend payments

97.   What describes a debt-equity ratio for a company?

    A. Profitability indicator
    B. Financial leverage indicator
    C. Liquidity indicator
    D. Market capitalization indicator

98.   What is underwriting?

    A. Evaluating insurance risks of specified individual/asset
    B. Guaranteeing new issue sales
    C. Rebalancing a portfolio
    D. Transferring securities between accounts

99.   What is Beta in investing?

A. Measurement of security volatility
B. A Greek letter
C. An earnings ratio
D. Bond

100. Which trading option is NOT a limit order instruction?

A. Trade at the current price
B. Buy at a specified price
C. Trade at a better price
D. Sell at a better price

101. What entitles a firm to become a corporation?

A. Registration of statement
B. Statement of additional information (SAI)
C. Corporate charter
D. Tabulation

102. Which of these is outlined in the SEC Rule 415?

A. Primary offerings
B. Shelf registration
C. Secondary offerings
D. IPOs

103. What is the cooling-off period for new issues?

A. 30 days
B. 20 days
C. 15 days
D. 60 days

104. All are TRUE for new issuance of securities EXCEPT:

    A. Matching orders
    B. Stabilization
    C. Due diligence
    D. Cooling-off period

105. Which is not in a tombstone ad?

    A. Syndicate members
    B. Syndicate managers
    C. The issuer
    D. The selling group

106. Which state security registration is valid for established businesses that sold state securities previously?

    A. Coordination
    B. Indemnification
    C. Notification
    D. Qualification

107. Which type of state securities registration is used for SEC-exempted securities but must have state registration?

    A. Indemnification
    B. Notification
    C. Coordination
    D. Qualification

108. The underwriter determines all EXCEPT:

    A. The takedown
    B. Public offering price
    C. Order allocation
    D. Effective date

109. What is the meaning of an offering becoming effective per SEC ruling?

   A. SEC verification
   B. SEC approval
   C. SEC clearance
   D. All of the above

110. Which Act covers the registration and disclosure requirements for new issues?

   A. Securities Act of 1933
   B. Trust Indenture Act of 1939
   C. Securities Exchange Act of 1934
   D. All of the above

111. Which document outlines the liabilities and responsibilities of issuing firms?

   A. Registration statement
   B. Letter of intent
   C. Code of conduct
   D. Syndicate agreement

112. Which document contains an order allocation?

   A. Trust indenture
   B. Syndicate agreement
   C. Preliminary prospectus
   D. Official statement

113. Which document specifies retaining of unsold securities by underwriters?

   A. Mini-max
   B. All-or-none (AON)
   C. Firm commitment
   D. Best efforts

114. Which is not a bond underwriting?

    A. Mini-max
    B. best efforts
    C. AON
    D. Standby

115. Which document must be signed by selling group members?

    A. Syndicate agreement
    B. Letter of intent
    C. Selling group agreement
    D. Repurchase agreement

116. At what price can stabilized bids be entered?

    A. Stabilizing price per final prospectus
    B. At or just above the public offering price
    C. At or little below the public offering price
    D. Federally determined price

117. The public offering price for a new issue is $1,000. The issuer gets $979/ bond. What is this $21 difference called?

    A. Underwriting spread
    B. Additional takedown
    C. Takedown
    D. Concession

118. What is the profit syndicate members make for selling new issues called?

    A. Concession
    B. Re-allowance
    C. Takedown
    D. Spread

119. Common stock is sold to a syndicate at $14/share during underwriting. The public offering price is $15/share, the manager charges $0.25/share, and the concession is $.80/share. What is the additional takedown?

    A. $0.45/share
    B. $0.75/share
    C. 41.25/share
    D. $1.50/share

120. What is the profit of the selling group if it sells an entire allotment of 500,000 of $2 million in new issues to the public by Kutchina Corp? Other values: Shares sold: 500,000, sale price to syndicate:$8/share, public offering: $9/share, takedown$0.80/share, concession:0.50/share, retaining charge for managing underwriter:0.15/share.

    A. $425,000
    B. $150,000
    C. $350,000
    D. $250,000

121. When may potential customers get a red herring?

    A. Before the issuer signs a registration statement
    B. Post-effective 45th-day
    C. Post-effective 60th-day
    D. Cooling-off period

122. Which is a must in the final prospectus?

    A. Offering price
    B. Issuer's income statement
    C. Issuer's balance sheet
    D. Issuer's income and balance sheets

123. How long must broker-dealers executing client orders for a firm's common stock issues through IPO have a copy of the final prospectus available after the effective date? The stocks will trade on the stock exchange when first issued.

    A. 90 days
    B. 65 days
    C. 70 days
    D. 50 days

124. Which offering is not SEC exempted?

    A. Private placements
    B. Limited partnership public offerings
    C. Auction-sold Treasury notes
    D. Rule 147 offerings

125. All are exempted under the Securities Act of 1933 EXCEPT:

    A. Treasury bonds
    B. REITs
    C. Public utility stocks
    D. Municipal General Obligation Bonds

Answer Key

Q.	1	2	3	4	5	6	7	8	9	10	11	12	13	14
A.	A	C	C	B	D	C	B	A	A	B	A	D	C	A

Q.	15	16	17	18	19	20	21	22	23	24	25	26	27	28
A.	C	iv	A	iii	D	D	B	B	B	A	A	A	C	D

Q.	29	30	31	32	33	34	35	36	37	38	39	40	41	42
A.	D	ii	A	B	B	C	C	iv	C	A	iv	A	iv	B

Q.	43	44	45	46	47	48	49	50	51	52	53	54	55	56
A.	A	ii	A	C	A	ii	B	i	A	C	B	D	D	A

Q.	57	58	59	60	61	62	63	64	65	66	67	68	69	70
A.	B	B	A	C	A	A	B	B	B	B	A	B	A	B

Q.	71	72	73	74	75	76	77	78	79	80	81	82	83	84
A.	B	B	C	C	A	B	C	D	C	B	D	A	B	C

Q.	85	86	87	88	89	90	91	92	93	94	95	96	97	98
A.	A	D	C	B	B	A	A	B	A	A	C	A	B	B

Q.	99	100	101	102	103	104	105	106	107	108	109	110	111	112
A.	A	A	C	B	B	A	D	C	D	D	C	A	D	B

Q.	113	114	115	116	117	118	119	120	121	122	123	124	125
A.	C	D	C	C	A	C	B	D	D	A	A	B	B

Answer Key and Explanations

1.   A. A principal's signature must be on all order tickets.

2.   C. Principals must approve trades on the same day as execution. It may not be before execution.

3.   C. Corporate bonds settle in two business days.

4.   B. Corporate bonds pay in four business days after trading.

5.   D. For stocks, the settlement day is in two business days, but payment is 4 business days after the trade date.

6.   C. Municipal bonds take two business days to settle.

7.   B. Payment is due in two business days after the trade date for munis.

8.   A. US government bond transactions settle in one business day following the trade date or T+1.

9.   A. Options trade settle in T+1 business date.

10.   B. Cash trades settle on the T date. Regular way settlement happens on T+2. Consider the weekend for the actual settlement.

11.   A. A "Don't know" (DK) notice is a trading term for inconsistent transaction information. A "don't know" deal occurs when one party challenges or rejects the trade for whatever reason, such as a price or share discrepancy. The Automated Confirmation Transaction Act manages it.

12.   D. All these organizations can grant an extension for the payment of a trade..

13.   C. If a client fails to pay for the trade by the payment date, the security is sold out, and the account is frozen.

14.   A. Before the purchase order may be executed, the client must pay the full purchase price of the securities.

15.   C. Every member firm must send a trade confirmation to a client at or before each transaction completion.

16.   iv. The client confirmation has the trade and settlement date, the security's name and type, the number of traded shares, and the amount of the agency's commission.

17.   A. For a member-to-client transaction, the member firm must send trade confirmation at or before completing the transaction.

18.   iii. A confirmation includes the amount charged, the commission, the security description, the registered rep's ID, etc. The markup or markdown is not disclosed for principal transactions.

19.   D. MSRB rules mandate confirmations regarding whether a trade was done on a principal (dealer) or agency (broker) basis.

20.   D. The address of the brokerage firm doesn't feature in the trade confirmation.

21.   B. For member-to-member transactions, the firms must send trade confirmation no later than one business day after the settlement dates.

22.   B. Brokerage firms cannot validate mutilated certificates.

23.   B. Securities cannot be rejected because their market price has changed.

24.   A. The number of shares on each certificate is in multiples of 100, divisors of 100, or in units that can add up to 100.

25.   A. Reclamation is returning previously accepted securities.

26.   A. Rejection is a refusal of securities at the time of delivery.

27. C. Puts are one of the best ways to hedge a long stock position against a market downturn.

28. D. Bond counsel examines new municipal issues for legality, validity, and tax exemption. They examine municipal, state, judicial, and tax laws to do so. Except for their comprehensive anti-fraud provisions, the Securities Act does not apply to municipal, government, or agency securities, so bond counsel would not review it for legal advice.

29. D. If a client sells securities but fails to deliver them within 10 business days after the settlement date, the firm must procure them from another seller.

30. ii. The stock purchaser receives a due bill from the issuer if purchasing before the ex-dividend date. The trade settles after the record date due to delayed delivery.

31. A. DRS allows investors to keep stock or bond certificates in book entry form.

32. B. The registrar is responsible for ensuring that issued shares do not exceed authorized shares, not the transfer agent.

33. B. Whether active or inactive, clients must receive account statements at least once every three months or quarterly.

34. C. If a question does not mention whether the account is active or inactive, it must be considered inactive, and the client should receive quarterly statements. For active clients, statements pertain to the traded month.

35. C. Mutual funds send account statements semiannually.

36. iv. Account statements per FINRA and SEC standards must be sent to clients at least quarterly for active and inactive accounts and semiannually for mutual funds.

37. C. The ex-dividend date is Wednesday, September 16, a day before Thursday, September 17.

38. A. The ex-dividend date comes one business day before the record date.

39. iv. The declaration date of the dividend is followed by the ex-dividend date. The record date follows when the business inspects its books to see which investors will be paid. The dividend is finally paid on the payment date.

40. A. The last day to buy stock regularly and receive dividends is Monday, October 15, the business day before the ex-dividend date.

41. iv. The seller can sell the stocks on Wednesday, August 14, or Friday 16, on a cash basis.

42. B. The firm must acknowledge receiving the complaint and document any action to resolve it.

43. A. Most firms make the client sign an arbitration agreement. If not, the client can decide whether to settle a dispute through COP or arbitration. They may appeal if they are discontented with the outcome.

44. ii. Non-members or clients may take members to arbitration, and arbitration decisions are binding and non-appealable.

45. A. Members cannot take non-members to arbitration.

46. C. The value for simplified arbitration used for member-to-non-member disputes should not exceed $50,000.

47. A. Arbitration decisions are less costly than court actions and must be complied with within 15 days of notification.

48. ii. Arbitration decisions are binding, but mediation decisions are not binding and can be appealed.

49. B. A brokerage firm must be a member of the National Securities Clearing Corporation (NSCC) to process an ACAT.

50. i. Account transfers between brokerages follow a receipt of ACAT notice. Firms must verify the client's instructions within one business day and transfer assets within three business days after verifications.

51. A. Rule G-39 states that cold calls must be made after 8 am and before 9 pm, depending on the client's local time.

52. C. They cannot be contacted before five years.

53. B. The 5% markup policy states that a brokerage firm can apply all relevant trade factors to determine the markup or commission charged to a client. The exception is the dealer cost.

54. D. The 5% markup policy is not for primary offerings, mutual funds, or Regulation D offerings.

55. D. For the execution of outstanding securities, public broker-dealers must use the 5% markup policy.

56. A. Equity = (Credit Balance - Short Market Value)

57. B. Municipal broker-dealers who understand municipal markets advise municipalities. The financial adviser charges a municipality for helping it prepare a competitive bid offering. The advising company seeks the lowest interest rate for the issuer. Underwriting by the same business creates a conflict of interest. The underwriter wants the issuer's highest interest rate to make selling easier.

58. B. Options website provide options "advertising" per the Securities Act of 1933.

59.   A. Quantitative easing is a non-traditional policy of buying securities by the Central Bank to increase the money supply. QI lowers short-term interest rates, and the prices of these financial assets will rise, increasing investments.

60.   C. The principal role of the Federal Reserve is to control money supply and interest rates.

61.   A. It's possible to convert a convertible bond into the issuing firm's stock.

62.   A. A margin call is a broker's demand for investors to deposit additional money/assets to cover likely losses.

63.   B. It is an employer-sponsored retirement saving plan.

64.   B. Initial Public Offering

65.   B. A stop-loss order is given to mitigate losses at or after a certain price.

66.   B. An option gives the holder the right (but not obligation) to trade an asset at an agreed price under specified conditions.

67.   A. In a primary market, the investor buys issues directly from the issuing company.

68.   B. A Closed-end fund releases a fixed share number through an IPO.

69.   A. EBITDA: Earnings Before Interest, Taxes, Depreciation, and Amortization measures the company's operational performance.

70.   B. A hedge fund employs various strategies to earn active interest.

71.   B. The P/E ratio, an evaluation, refers to the Price to Earnings ratio.

72.   B. Insider trading is based on confidential, non-public information and is prohibited.

73. C. A junk bond is below investment grade with higher yields.

74. C. Short selling is selling borrowed shares intending to repurchase them at a lower price.

75. A. Day trading involves multiple shares trading on the same day to maximize profits.

76. B. An annuity is a series of regular dividends for retirement plans.

77. C. ROI: Return on Investment, measures investment profitability.

78. D. An illiquid asset is difficult to procure and sell at its right price.

79. C. A bid price is the price at which the investor is willing to purchase.

80. B. Blue chip stocks are stocks from a large company.

81. D. A put option is the holder's right (but not obligation) to sell stocks at a specified price before a given date.

82. A. Market capitalization represents a firm's overall stock market worth.

83. B. A coupon rate is the annual interest paid to bondholders.

84. C. Preferred stocks pay more dividends than regular stocks but usually do not have voting rights.

85. A. An index is a benchmark of performance of various assets/asset classes.

86. D. An alpha is a benchmark that assesses the extent of securities performance for its market index.

87. C. Growth stocks are expected to grow above average compared to other market stocks.

88. B. A day trader trades securities within the same day.

89. B. Unethical trading is inside trading.

90. A. Leverage involves risk but aims to increase profits by using borrowed money to raise returns.

91. A. A limit order is an order to trade at a precise price or better

92. B. IPO enables a firm to go public to raise capital.

93. A. A bid-ask spread is the difference between the maximum price a buyer can pay and the lowest the bidder offers.

94. A. Dollar-cost averaging is investing a fixed amount regularly irrespective of asset price.

95. C. On the initial transaction on a margin account, an investor must pay the RgT amount (50% of purchase)/$2000 (for a long margin account)/ full payment. So, he must either pay $1000 or $2000. The answer choices do not mention $1000.

96. A. A no-interest bond, the zero-coupon bond is traded at a discount to its face value and matures at face value.

97. B. A debt-equity ratio indicates a firm's financial leverage.

98. B. Underwriting is an investment bank's guarantee to sell a firm's new issues to provide liquidity and raise capital.

99. A. Beta in investing is a measurement of security volatility.

100. A. Current price trading isn't a limit order instruction.

101. C. Firms must file a corporate charter in their home state of business to become a corporation.

102. B. SEC rule 415 outlines shelf registration.

103. B. During cooling-off, the SEC reviews a company's registration before releasing new issues.

104. A. Except for matching orders, the rest apply to the issuance of new securities.

105. D. A tombstone ad announces the issuance of new issues; it doesn't have the names of selling group members.

106. C. Companies that have already sold securities in a state can renew their previous notification registration.

107. D. Qualification needed on the state level is exempted by the SEC.

108. D. SEC determines the effective date.

109. C. Effective issue means SEC clearance.

110. A. The Securities Act (1933).

111. D. The syndicate agreement, signed by all members, describes the responsibilities and liabilities of the members.

112. B. The syndicate agreement has an allocation of orders (customer order prioritization) per MSRB rules.

113. C. Firm commitment underwriting contains any unsold securities retained by the underwriters.

114. D. Standby underwriting is for ordinary stockholders.

115. C. Selling group members must sign the selling group agreement.

116. C. Stabilizing bids cannot raise the issue's market price and must be at or just below the public offering price.

117. A. The underwriting spread is the difference between the public offering price and what the issuer gets (or takedown + the manager's charges).

118. C. Takedown is a syndicate member's profit for selling shares of a new issue.

119. B. Additional takedown is the profit made by syndicate members on shares sold by the selling group. First, determine the spread = (public offering price – syndicate amount / share). Or, $15 – $14 = $1. Takedown = (spread – manager's fees). Or, $1 – $0.25 = $0.75

120. D. The selling group retains the concession. Thus, selling 500,000 shares means the total is 500,000 × (0.50) = $250,000.

121. D. Potential customers may get a red herring, the preliminary prospectus, during the cooling-off period.

122. A. The final prospectus has the final offering price, among other vital information.

123. A. To trade an initial public offering on the Over-the-Counter Bulletin Board (OTCBB/OTCPink) market, brokerage firms executing orders for customers to acquire the stock must provide a receipt of trade within 90 days after the effective date.

124. B. Limited partnership public offerings are not SEC exempted.

125. B. REITs must register with the Securities Act.

Chapter Eight: Practice Test III

You have three hours to complete the 125 questions in this test.

1.   Which is not a fixed asset?

    A. Computers
    B. Office furniture
    C. Inventory
    D. Warehouse

2.   Sally, a 55-year investor, wants to add some liquidity to her portfolio. All these are suitable EXCEPT?

    A. An oil and gas limited partnership
    B. Treasury bills
    C. Blue chip stocks
    D. Aggressive growth fund

3.   What is the advantage of investing in a direct participation program (DPP)?

    A. Pass through of income and losses
    B. Professional management
    C. Limited liability
    D. All of the above

4. Which is true for a limited partner helping a general partner acquire investors for a partnership?

   A. May harm the limited partner's position
   B. Permissible if mentioned in the limited partnership agreement
   C. Permissible, provided the limited partner is not compensated
   D. None of the above

5. All are responsibilities for the general partner of a hospital developmental partnership EXCEPT:

   A. Handling partnership expenses
   B. Controlling partnerships
   C. Approving new limited partnership
   D. Giving most partnership capital

6. Who assumes maximum risk in a limited partnership?

   A. The general partner.
   B. The limited partner.
   C. It depends on the partnership terms.
   D. Both have the same amount of risk.

7. Which partnerships enable limited partners to deduct nonrecourse debt as a tax deduction?

   A. Oil and gas wildcatting
   B. Real estate
   C. Oil and gas developmental
   D. Equipment leasing

8. Which partnership documents must be filed with the SEC before making a public offering?

   A. Subscription agreement
   B. Limited partnership agreement
   C. Certificate of limited partnership

D. All of the above

9. Which investment requires written evidence of a client's net worth?

    A. An oil and gas limited partnership
    B. An aggressive growth fund
    C. A face-amount certificate company
    D. A variable annuity contract

10. Which document must a general partner sign to take a new limited partner?

    A. Subscription agreement
    B. Limited partnership agreement
    C. Certificate of limited partnership
    D. A prospectus

11. Which of the following may be mitigated by real estate DPP losses?

    A. Earned income
    B. Portfolio income
    C. Capital gains from REIT
    D. Income from oil and gas partnership

12. Which of the following doesn't describe limited partnership tax status?

    A. All generated income is taxed as ordinary income.
    B. Gains are taxed as capital gains.
    C. Limited and general partners share the tax.
    D. IRS taxes the full partnership.

13. A wealthy client wants to invest in a real estate partnership with income stability. Which one should you recommend?

    A. Section 8
    B. New construction
    C. Condominiums

D. Raw land

14. What is the prime concern of an investor in an undeveloped land-limited partnership?

    A. Cash flow
    B. Appreciation
    C. Depreciation
    D. Depletion

15. Which of the real estate DPPs have the least write-offs?

    A. Public housing
    B. Existing properties
    C. Raw land
    D. New construction

16. All are part of an equipment leasing partnership EXCEPT:

    A. Oil well drill heads
    B. Construction equipment
    C. Moving trucks
    D. Computers

17. Unless otherwise mentioned, which is represented by an underlying stock option contract?

    A. 100 shares
    B. 1000 shares
    C. 10,000 shares
    D. 10 shares

18. What is the expiration date for standard option contracts?

    A. Six months
    B. Nine months
    C. Twelve months

D. Forty months

19. Two days remain on an October 40 call option. The market stock value is 62. What is the likely premium?

   A. 16
   B. 2
   C. 22.50
   D. 0.754

20. A DKL call option premium increased by 0.75. What is the dollar amount of the raise?

   A. $750
   B. $75
   C. $0.75
   D. $7.50

21. A consumer expects DPS stock to decline in the coming months. Which investment strategy would capitalize on the expected downturn with the least cash?

   A. Purchasing a DPS straddle
   B. Buying a DPS put option
   C. Purchasing a DPS call option
   D. Shorting DPS stock

22. What is the underlying security's market price if a call option is in the money?

   A. Below is the strike price minus the premium
   B. Lower than the strike price
   C. Above the strike price
   D. Above the strike price plus the premium

23. Which option is out of money if the DBF is $40?

   A. DBF May 50 put
   B. DBF May 50 call
   C. DBF May 45 put
   D. DBF May 30 call

24. An RTW Nov 55 call is trading for 9 when RTW is at $60. What is the option's time value?

   A. 9
   B. 4
   C. 0
   D. 5

25. Which is the most hazardous option strategy?

   A. Selling uncovered calls
   B. Selling uncovered puts
   C. Buying calls
   D. Buying puts

26. An investor writes an FTJ Dec 60 call for 5. What is his maximum potential gain?

   A. $5,300
   B. $500
   C. $1,500
   D. $300

27. Without any positions, an investor writes a VHT Dec call at 5. What is this action?

   A. Closing sale
   B. Closing purchase
   C. Opening purchase
   D. Opening sale

28. A client purchases 100 shares at $45.10 and a 790 put at 4.50. After a few months, the stock value is $43.55, and the put is trading at 760. What is the profit if they close the stock position and exercise the put?

   A. $155
   B. $1,100
   C. $495
   D. $2,395

29. Which is a long straddle?

   A. Selling a call and selling a put
   B. Buying a put and selling a put
   C. Buying a call and selling a call
   D. Buying a call and buying a put

30. Which option strategy is suitable for a stock with a high beta?

   A. Long straddle
   B. Short combination
   C. Bullish spread
   D. Short a put

31. What should the trading price be for a mutual fund if an investor wants to redeem the shares?

   A. The next calculated ask price.
   B. The present ask price.
   C. The next calculated bid price.
   D. The present bid price.

32. An investor finds that a fund's NAV rose by $0.90 while its POP decreased by $0.30. What is this fund?

   A. Balanced
   B. No-load
   C. Closed-end

D. Open-end

33.   At what price does the redemption of mutual fund shares occur?

A. Current POP
B. Current NAV
C. Next-estimated POP
D. Next-estimated NAV

34.   Which is not true for open-end investment companies?

A. Money is not loaned to clients to buy shares.
B. The public offering price is never below the NAV.
C. Buyers are charged with commissions.
D. Public shares are continuously offered.

35.   What percentage of net investment income must an investment business deliver to shareholders to avoid corporate taxation?

A. 80%
B. 90%
C. 70%
D. 75%

36.   Which criterion must be satisfied for an investment company to be considered diversified?

A. The 75-5-10 test
B. The 80-5-5 test
C. The 70-5-10 test
D. The 80-20 test

37.   Which investment would be best for a married couple in their mid-20s paying maximum IRA contributions?

A. Buying index call options
B. Commodities

C. DPPs

D. Growth funds

38. Which securities type is least suitable for a client mainly interested in current income?

    A. An income fund

    B. A muni

    C. A high-yield bond

    D. A sector fund investing in high-tech stocks

39. What is a mutual fund type that holds a security portfolio consisting of a corporation's stocks while releasing new products?

    A. Life-cycle fund

    B. Dual-purpose fund

    C. Special situation fund

    D. Specialized fund

40. Which fund do you recommend to a customer investing $450/month in mutual funds? They want a low-risk fund as they age.

    A. Tax-free muni fund

    B. Money market fund

    C. Aggressive growth fund

    D. Life-cycle fund

41. Which mutual fund provides safe, tax-free income?

    A. A money market fund

    B. A high-yield bond fund

    C. A fund of hedge funds

    D. An insured muni bond fund

42. Which is best for a client in the top federal income tax bracket?

    A. A muni

B. US government bond fund
C. Aggressive growth fund
D. Money market fund

43.   What is the maximum sales charge for mutual funds?

A. NAV 6%
B. NAV 8.5%
C. The investment amount's 5%
D. The investment amount's 7%

44.   What is the POP of mutual funds?

A. Net asset value/sales charge
B. Net asset value × sales charge
C. Net asset value – sales charge
D. Net asset value + sales charge

45.   What is the sales percentage for the DARCO growth fund with an NAV value of $9.50 and a POP of $10?

A. 5%
B. 2.5%
C. 4%
D. 10%

46.   Which is advantageous for investors who want to hold long-term muni funds?

A. Class C load
B. Class B load
C. Class A load
D. Class D load

47.   Which investment type is most similar to a zero-coupon bond?

A. Face-amount certificate company

B. Closed-end fund

C. Open-end fund

D. Unit investment trust

48. Which investment doesn't charge management fees and invests in a fixed securities portfolio?

A. Face-amount certificate company

B. REIT

C. Unit investment trust (UIT)

D. Mutual fund

49. For exchange-traded funds, all are TRUE(ETFs) EXCEPT:

A. Securities are redeemable

B. New securities are offered only once

C. Subjected to short-selling

D. Traded in exchange or over-the-counter

50. Which step is appropriate for a client who is bearish on the market?

A. A hedge fund

B. An inverse exchange-traded fund

C. Index fund short-selling

D. Dual-purpose short selling

51. Which security type is actively traded in the secondary market?

A. REITs

B. Unit investment trust

C. Open-end funds

D. All of these

52. Which is not a REIT?

A. Double-barreled

B. Mortgage

C. Equity

D. Hybrid

53. What percentage of profits must REITs distribute to avoid being taxed as a corporation?

A. 85%

B. 90%

C. 65%

D. 55%

54. All are covered by the Investment Company Act of 1940 EXCEPT:

A. Variable annuities

B. Closed-end funds

C. Fixed annuities

D. Open-end funds

55. Who assumes the investment risk in a variable annuity?

A. Policyholder

B. The insurance company holds 60%; the policyholder holds 40%

C. The policyholder

D. None of them

56. All are valid for variable annuities EXCEPT:

A. Investors are safeguarded against capital loss.

B. Separately held accounts are managed professionally.

C. Separate securities accounts can be mutual funds.

D. Unlike fixed annuities, they are more likely to vary with inflation.

57. A 28-year-old investor received a vast inheritance and wants to invest in a variable annuity. Which purchasing option would be the best for this investor?

A. Single payment deferred annuity

B. Single payment immediate annuity
C. Immediate annuity with deferred payment
D. Periodic payment deferred annuity

58. If your client wants the variable annuity to provide the largest monthly income, which option would suit him the best?

    A. Life income annuity
    B. Joint and last survivor annuity
    C. Life with period certain annuity
    D. Sufficient information is lacking

59. Which variable annuity type would guarantee life payment?

    A. Deferred guarantee
    B. Mortality guarantee
    C. Post-payment guarantee
    D. Life-payment guarantee

60. Which variable annuity types pay the largest monthly payment to annuitants?

    A. Unit refund
    B. Life annuity with period certain
    C. Straight life annuity
    D. Joint and survivor annuity

61. All are likely 1035 tax-free exchanges EXCEPT:

    A. Whole life to fixed annuities
    B. Whole life to universal life
    C. Variable annuity to variable life insurance
    D. Fixed annuity to variable annuity

62. What is the most vital consideration when making client recommendations?

    A. Investment objectives

B. Marital status

C. Financial requirements

D. Age

63.   A new client with a long-term objective of aggressive growth plans to purchase a fixer-upper home in a year. What should be best suitable for their portfolio?

A. An oil and gas wildcatting program

B. High-yield bond fund

C. Treasury bills

D. Aggressive growth funds

64.   Which is good for capital growth?

A. REITs

B. Munis

C. T-bonds

D. New corporation's stock

65.   A newly investing client with $15,000 wants to create a diversified portfolio. Which is the best recommendation?

A. Three types of bonds and several blue chip stocks.

B. A diversified portfolio can't be built with $15,000.

C. Purchase T-bonds and slowly add stocks with the received interests.

D. Purchase various mutual funds.

66.   What would you recommend to a client with 100% portfolio investment in common stocks and common stock mutual funds if they have a total return objective?

A. Corporate bonds

B. Preferred stocks

C. Aggressive growth mutual funds

D. Blue chip stocks

67. Which of these must be obtained before making a client recommendation?

    A. Obtaining the client's written power of attorney
    B. The principal's written approval
    C. Client's suitability
    D. All of these

68. Which nonfinancial conditions of a client must be checked before making an investment recommendation?

    A. Age
    B. Employment status
    C. Marital status
    D. All of these

69. What should be the tactical asset allocation if an investor feels that the market will be going on a run over the short term?

    A. Buy more short-term debt securities; sell some long-term debt securities.
    B. Buy more fixed-income securities; sell some equity securities.
    C. Buy some equity securities; sell some fixed-income securities.
    D. Buy more precious metals; sell some debt and equity securities.

70. Which is valid for a pharma company with negative alpha?

    A. It is underperforming other stocks on the S&P 100.
    B. It is underperforming similar pharmaceutical stocks.
    C. It is underperforming the return on the DJIA.
    D. It is underperforming other stocks on the S&P 500.

71. What does purchasing a stock with a beta of 1.6 mean?

    A. A more volatile stock than others
    B. Less volatile than others
    C. As volatile as others
    D. None of these

72.   Jane Williams, a client, pursues an aggressive stock-purchasing strategy. Which investment should best suit her?

A. UNH stock with a beta coefficient of 1.30
B. LTR stock with a beta of 1
C. Blue chip stock
D. GTH stock with beat 0f 0.70

73.   Which of these describes a systematic risk?

A. The issuer won't perform per expectations.
B. Security won't keep pace with the inflation rate.
C. The issuer may default.
D. Security can decline due to adverse market conditions.

74.   Which investment option is best for an investor concerned about interest risk?

A. Treasury bonds
B. Treasury STRIPS
C. Treasury bills
D. Treasury notes

75.   What is the main risk for a client who owns a large amount of Treasury bonds and long-term investment-grade corporate bonds?

A. Timing risk
B. Inflation
C. Systemic risk
D. Credit risk

76.   If the FDA raises pollution standards that are more expensive for oil companies, what is the likely reason for declining oil company stock shares?

A. Regulatory risk
B. Reinvestment risk
C. Credit risk

D. Purchasing power risk

77. Which debt security is without reinvestment risk?

   A. Treasury STRIPS
   B. Equipment trusts
   C. Municipal GO bonds
   D. Industrial development revenue bonds

78. A 57-year-old investor has a $100,000 investment and wants to add more liquid securities. Which choice suits him best?

   A. Treasury bills
   B. Mutual funds
   C. Blue chip stocks
   D. DPPs

79. Which is not analyzed by a fundamental analyst?

   A. Industry
   B. Balance sheets
   C. EPS
   D. Timing

80. A technical analyst considers all these while assessing a corporation's stock EXCEPT:

   A. Market momentum
   B. The corporation's earnings
   C. The market price
   D. The trading volume

81. Which of these corporation features does a fundamental analyst examine?

   A. Breadth of the market
   B. Support and resistance
   C. Earnings trend

D. None of these

82.   All are current assets EXCEPT:

A. Receivable accounts
B. Machinery
C. Securities
D. Cash

83.   Which is not a quick asset?

A. Inventory
B. Marketable securities
C. Cash
D. Accounts receivable

84.   Which is an unethical practice?

A. Matching orders
B. Stabilization
C. Due diligence
D. Cooling-off period

85.   How would you determine the net worth of a corporation?

A. Liabilities + assets
B. Stockholder equities – assets
C. Liabilities – assets
D. Assets – liabilities

86.   What is working capital?

A. Net worth – liabilities
B. Liabilities + stockholder equities
C. Asset – liabilities
D. Current assets – current liabilities

87. What happens to KJH's working capital before and after announcing $0.60 dividends to holders of record of their common stock?

    A. It decreases.
    B. It rises.
    C. It remains the same.
    D. It cannot be determined.

88. What happens to a company's net worth while issuing common stock?

    A. It remains unaffected.
    B. It rises.
    C. It decreases.
    D. It is undetermined.

89. Which indicator determines a corporation's bankruptcy risk?

    A. Debt-to-equity ratio
    B. Margin of profit ratio
    C. Inventory turnover ratio
    D. Net profit ratio

90. What is cash flow?

    A. Gross income – depletion + depreciation
    B. Gross income + depletion + depreciation
    C. Net income + depletion + depreciation + amortization
    D. Net income – depreciation

91. If BPH common stock has a $2.50 dividend, a current yield of 5%, and a PE ratio of 5. It is trading at $50. What is the approximate earnings per share (EPS)?

    A. $10
    B. $6
    C. $7.50
    D. $0.68

92. ASZ stock gives an annual dividend of $5, earnings/share of $10, and a market price of $60. What is its PE ratio?

    A. 2
    B. 6
    C. 7
    D. 9

93. Where would you obtain the data for first-in-first-out (FIFO) inventory valuation?

    A. Customer's account statement
    B. The corporation's statement for additional information
    C. Footnotes of the corporation's balance sheet
    D. Balance sheet

94. Which theory is based on the idea that investors typically buy and sell at the wrong time?

    A. Short interest theory
    B. Modern portfolio theory
    C. Odd-lot theory
    D. Random walk theory

95. Which confirms the reversal of a bearish trend per Dow theory?

    A. Rise in investors buying call options
    B. Advance/decline ratio
    C. The amount of short interest
    D. Increase in Dow Jones Industrial Average (DJIA) and Dow Jones Transportation Average (DJTA)

96. What is happening to UJC stock, which was very volatile over the past two years but now trades consistently between $50 and $51?

    A. Consolidating
    B. Breaking out

C. Saucering
D. Trend lining

97. What is a head and shoulders top formation?

A. Security awaits breakout
B. Consolidating security
C. Reversal of bullish trends
D. Reversal of bearish trends

98. What is the correct step for an overbought market?

A. Sell index put options.
B. Buy index call options.
C. Buy securities.
D. Sell or sell short securities.

99. Which best describes a third market?

A. Listed securities trading OTC
B. Unlisted securities trading OTC
C. Listed securities trading on an exchange
D. Institutional trading

100. What is a securities trade between a bank and an insurance company without a broker-dealer service?

A. First market trade
B. Third market trade
C. Fourth market trade
D. Second market trade

101. Where do US Treasury bonds and munis trade?

A. OTC
B. On the NYSE
C. Either OTC or NYSE

D. Neither of the two

102.   Which NASDAQ level includes subject quotes?

A. Level IV
B. Level II
C. Level III
D. Level I

103.   Where would one find the most speculative securities on the OTC market?

A. Venture market
B. Pink sheets
C. Best market
D. Over-the-counter bulletin board (OTCBB)

104.   Which option is true?

A. Brokers charge commission; dealers take markup or markdown.
B. Both charge a markup or markdown.
C. Dealers charge commission; brokers take markup or markdown.
D. Both charge a commission.

105.   What is the role of the broker-dealer in making a market in a particular security?

A. Syndicate member
B. Broker
C. Agent
D. Principal

106.   What is the responsibility of a muni trader at a brokerage firm?

A. Underwriting new issue
B. Positioning clients of the firm
C. Rating the muni in the firm's inventory
D. All of these

107. What does regulation SHO cover?

    A. Securities short sale
    B. Portfolio margin rules
    C. Margin requirements for commodities
    D. Margin requirements for municipal and US government securities

108. Which becomes a market order when the underlying security passes a particular price?

    A. Stop
    B. Stop limit
    C. Market
    D. Limit

109. Which options guarantee the order is executed at a specific price or better?

    A. Buy stops, sell stops.
    B. Buy limits, sell stops.
    C. Sell limits, buy stops.
    D. Buy limits, sell limits.

110. Warren placed an order to purchase 1,200 shares at 32. What did he place?

    A. Market order
    B. Buy a stop limit order
    C. Buy a stop order
    D. Buy a limit order

111. Which of these a designated market maker (DMM) cannot accept?

    A. All-or-none (AON)
    B. Fill-or-kill (FOK)
    C. Not held (NH)
    D. Immediate-or-cancel (IOC)

112. Mr. Gomez owns 100 common stock shares with a market price of $40. He entered an order to sell these at $35 stop or sell at $45. What is the order type?

    A. An alternative order
    B. A fill-or-kill order
    C. A sell-limit order
    D. A sell-stop limit order

113. Who is responsible for maintaining a fair market on the NYSE trading floor?

    A. Order book officials
    B. Floor brokers
    C. Two-dollar brokers
    D. Designated market makers (DMM)

114. A client has entered an open order to sell 12,000 shares at $24; the business announced a 2-for-5 split. How will the DMM adjust the order on the ex-split date?

    A. The order would be canceled
    B. Sell 400 shares at $50
    C. Sell 20,000 shares at $8
    D. Sell 12,000 shares at $24

115. What does an Order Audit Trail System track?

    A. The entire life of an order
    B. Cancellation of an order
    C. Execution of an order
    D. None of the above

116. What computer system do broker-dealers use to track the routing of OTC orders?

    A. Order Audit Trail System (OATS)
    B. Electronic communication network (ECN)

C. Super display book (SDBK)

D. Automated Confirmation Transaction Service (ACT)

117. In which of these situations for the previous day's close will the NYSE temporarily halt trading?

    A. DJIA declines 5% or more
    B. DJIA declines 7% or more
    C. S&P declines 5% or more
    D. S&P declines 7% or more

118. For how many years must a broker-dealer keep corporate or partnership documents?

    A. Lifelong
    B. Six years
    C. Ten years
    D. Two years

119. What violation does a dealer make by failing to honor a firm quote?

    A. Commingling
    B. Freeriding
    C. Backing away
    D. Marking the open

120. All are violations EXCEPT:

    A. Entering an "at open order"
    B. Painting the tape
    C. Frontrunning
    D. Paying for referrals

121. For how long must complaints be maintained on brokerage firm records per FINRA?

    A. Ten years

B. Four years
C. Two years
D. Six years

122. All should be on the brokerage firm's records for at least six years, EXCEPT:

A. Blotters
B. Ledgers
C. Closed accounts
D. U-forms of terminated employees

123. How long should all required records be maintained in an easily accessible way per FINRA and MSRB rules?

A. Three years
B. Six years
C. Two years
D. Six months

124. When must a control relationship be disclosed to a potential security buyer per MSRB?

A. Recommendation time
B. Before transaction completion
C. At transaction completion
D. At or before transaction completion

125. A client gets a $2,500 cash dividend for securities held in a long-margin account. What dividend component will go to a special memorandum account (SMA)?

A. $2,000
B. $0
C. $2,500
D. $70

Answer Key

Q.	1	2	3	4	5	6	7	8	9	10	11	12	13	14
A.	C	A	D	A	D	A	B	C	A	A	D	D	A	B

Q.	15	16	17	18	19	20	21	22	23	24	25	26	27	28
A.	C	A	A	B	C	B	B	C	D	D	A	B	D	D

Q.	29	30	31	32	33	34	35	36	37	38	39	40	41	42
A.	D	A	C	C	D	C	B	A	D	D	C	D	D	A

Q.	43	44	45	46	47	48	49	50	51	52	53	54	55	56
A.	B	D	A	C	A	C	A	B	A	A	B	C	A	A

Q.	57	58	59	60	61	62	63	64	65	66	67	68	69	70
A.	A	A	B	C	C	A	C	D	D	A	C	D	C	B

Q.	71	72	73	74	75	76	77	78	79	80	81	82	83	84
A.	A	A	D	C	B	A	A	D	D	B	C	B	A	A

Q.	85	86	87	88	89	90	91	92	93	94	95	96	97	98
A.	C	D	A	B	A	C	A	B	C	C	D	A	C	D

Q.	99	100	101	102	103	104	105	106	107	108	109	110	111	112
A.	A	C	A	D	B	A	D	B	A	A	D	D	C	A

Q.	113	114	115	116	117	118	119	120	121	122	123	124	125
A.	D	A	A	A	D	A	C	A	B	D	C	A	C

Answer Key and Explanations

1.   C. Inventory is a current asset.

2.   A. Limited partnership is one of the most difficult to manage and unsuitable for investors looking for liquidity.

3.   D. All the options benefit investing in a DPP.

4.   A. A limited partner managing things for a general partner could lose their limited liability status.

5.   D. The limited partner provides the majority of the capital.

6.   A. The general partner bears the maximum risk.

7.   B. Nonrecourse debt is available only to limited partners in real estate DPPs.

8.   C. A Limited partnership must file a certificate of limited partnership with the SEC before the public offering.

9.   A. Limited partnership requires evidence of clients' financial conditions.

10.   A. General partner must sign a subscription agreement to accept a new limited partner.

11.   D. Passive losses can be mitigated only through passive gains from another DPP per IRS rules.

12.   D. The partnership is fully taxed.

13.   A. Investment in Section 8 would give a stable income.

14.   B. Appreciation is the prime concern of an investor in an undeveloped land-limited partnership.

15. C. DPP isn't spending money on developing the land, which doesn't depreciate. Hence, raw land DPPs have the least write-offs.

16. A. Oil well drill heads are not included in the equipment leasing partnership.

17. A. Most option contracts refer to the underlying security's 100 shares.

18. B. The expiration of standard option contracts is nine months.

19. C. Options premium (P) comprises intrinsic value (I) and time value (T). being a 40-call option, the I value is 22 (stock is at 62). Call options go in the money when the stock's price is above the strike price. Thus, the P must be at least 22. The T is small (2 days from expiry). Of the choices, the one that works is option c.

20. B. Option contracts refer to the underlying security's 100 shares. Thus 100 × 0.75 = 75.

21. B. Buying a put is a bearish option. For a modest investment, investors can be interested in a large amount of securities.

22. C. Call options go in the money when the stock's price exceeds the strike price.

23. D. The DBF May 30 call is out of money as the stock's price is below the strike price.

24. D. P = (I+T). Or, T = I − P. Or, T = 5

25. A. Selling uncovered calls is the most hazardous strategy because call options only go in money when the stock price exceeds the strike price.

26. B. There is no mention of other stock or option positions for this investor. As he sold the option, he could hope to retrieve the premium or $500 (5 P × 100 shares/option).

27. D. Trading in an option for the first time is an "opening transaction." the investor wrote it, making it an opening sale.

28. D. Let's calculate the money out and the money in and find the difference to have the profit.

Money Out	Money in
$4,510 ($45.10 × 100 shares)	$4,355 ($43.55 × 100 shares)
$450 ($4.50 × 100 shares/option)	$3,000 ($30 × 100 shares/option)
Total: $4,960	Total: $7,355

[To obtain option selling price (it was sold for cash): (Selling price – Strike price)

790 – 760 = 30],

The profit:

$7,355 – $4,960 = $2,395

29. D. Long means to buy.

30. A. A stock with a high beta is volatile and requires a long straddle.

31. C. Investors sell at the bid price, the NAV, for mutual funds.

32. C. The fund is a closed-end fund when NAV and POP move in opposite directions.

33. D. Mutual funds redemption and purchase occur at the next calculated NAV and POP.

34. C. Mutual funds don't charge commissions. A sales charge is added to the NAV.

35. B. Under Subchapter M, a regulated investment company (RIC) must "pass through" at least 90% of its net investments to shareholders to avoid being taxed as a corporation.

36.   A. A diversified investment company meets the 75-5-10 test.

37.   D. Young investors can take more risks. Growth funds with diversified portfolios have capital appreciation potential.

38.   D. Growth funds like high-tech stocks don't pay dividends and aren't suitable for current income.

39.   C. Special situation funds are firm stocks that release new products, have pending patents, have new management, etc.

40.   D. Life-cycle funds adjust the security portfolio by themselves. Investors must choose one with a target retirement date corresponding to their requirements.

41.   D. An insured muni has a high safety grade and is tax-free.

42.   A. Being tax-free, municipal bonds benefit investors in high-income tax brackets.

43.   B. The maximum sales charge for a mutual fund is 8.5% of the amount invested.

44.   D. The POP is NAV + sales charge.

45.   A. Sales charge% = (POP − NAV) / POP. 10 − 9.50/10. Or, 5%.

46.   C. Class A load is advantageous for investors who want to hold long-term muni funds.

47.   A. Face amount certificates, like zero-coupon bonds, guarantee a fixed amount (the face amount) at a predetermined date and pay no interim dividends.

48.   C. UITs don't have a supervising manager; they are fixed portfolio securities.

49. A. ETFs are closed-end funds and are not redeemable.

50. B. Inverse ETFs (short funds) hedge portfolios against falling prices.

51. A. Except for REITs, the rest don't trade in the secondary market.

52. A. REITs are of three types: Equity, mortgage, and hybrid; double-barreled is not a REIT.

53. B. REITs must distribute 90% of profits to avoid being taxed as a corporation.

54. C. The Investment Company Act doesn't cover fixed annuities.

55. A. The policyholder bears investment risks in a variable annuity.

56. A. Investors are not safeguarded against capital loss in variable annuities.

57. A. Single payment deferred annuity is the best option for this young investor with a large capital.

58. A. A Life income annuity has the highest monthly payments, which stop with the annuitant's death.

59. B. Variable annuity guarantees life payment.

60. C. Straight-life annuities without beneficiaries pay the largest monthly payment.

61. C. Switch from variable annuity to variable life insurance. Investors cannot switch money from annuities to life insurance without paying taxes.

62. A. Clients' investment objectives are the most vital considerations while making recommendations.

63. C. Treasury bills are safe, given the circumstances.

64. D. Speculative investors wanting to gain capital should invest in the stock of new corporations.

65. D. Purchasing various mutual funds is the only possibility for a client to have a diversified portfolio with $15,000.

66. A. Total return means growth and income. The client's current investment status is growth-based. Adding fixed-income securities like corporate bonds is helpful.

67. C. The client's business objective and suitability are the two most important considerations.

68. D. All the clauses are vital.

69. C. Tactical asset allocation involves rebalancing the portfolio per market conditions. If the stock market is expected to go on the run over the short term, the option is to buy some stock and sell some fixed-income securities.

70. B. A negative alpha, a performance benchmark, shows how the stock is performing compared to all similar pharmaceutical stocks. In this case, it is underperforming.

71. A. Beta measures stock volatility. Beta 1 means equally volatile stock to others in the market; Beta less than 1 indicates more volatility.

72. A. UNH stock with a beta coefficient of 1.30 indicates it will move more with the market, which suits the client's objectives.

73. D. Systematic risk or market risk means that securities decline due to adverse market conditions.

74. C. Short-term bonds like T-bills have low price volatility and low-interest risk.

75. B. All long-term bonds have inflationary or purchasing power risk.

76. A. Regulatory risk is declining security prices due to regulations on specific businesses.

77. A. Treasury STRIPS are issued at a discount and mature at par value without paying interim dividends. Reinvestment risk is associated with receiving annual interest and dividends and is absent in Treasury STRIPS.

78. D. DPPs are not good liquidity choices because of the difficulty in procuring and selling them.

79. D. The technical analyst assesses the suitable timing for trading securities.

80. B. A technical analyst doesn't evaluate investment earnings.

81. C. Fundamental analysts assess the earnings trend, compare companies, and determine what to buy.

82. B. Machinery is a fixed asset. Current assets, including cash, securities, inventory, accounts receivable, and prepaid expenses, can easily be converted into cash within the next 12 months.

83. A. Quick assets like cash, accounts receivable, and securities can be converted into cash within 3–5 months.

84. A. Matching orders unethically manipulate securities prices to seem more active.

85. C. The net worth of a business = (Liabilities – assets).

86. D. Working capital = (Current assets –current liabilities).

87. A. Working capital decreases.

88. B. The net worth rises. The company receives cash, increasing net worth and working capital.

89. A. Debt-to-equity ratio and bond ratio help fundamental analysts determine the business' bankruptcy risks.

90. C. Cash flow = (Net income + depletion + depreciation + amortization).

91. A. EPS = Stock price / PE, (50/5) = 10

92. B. PE ratio = Market price/EPS, (60/10) = 6

93. C. Footnotes of the corporation's balance sheet give investors an idea of the issuer's accounting procedures.

94. C. The odd-lot theory proposes that investors buy and sell at the wrong time.

95. D. An increase in The DJIA and DJTA indicates a reversal of bearish trends.

96. A. The stock is consolidating.

97. C. It indicates a reversal of bullish trends.

98. D. The correct step is to sell or sell short securities.

99. A. Third market trade is listed securities trading OTC.

100. C. It is a fourth market trade.

101. A. US Treasury bonds and munis trade on OTC.

102. D. NASDAQ level I includes subject quotes.

103. B. OTC pink sheets are the most speculative securities on the market.

104. A. Brokers charge commission; dealers take markup or markdown.

105. D. A broker-dealer making a market in a particular security is a market maker or principal.

106. B. The trading department helps with positioning or buying and selling of securities.

107. A. Regulation SHO regulates short sales.

108. A. Stop orders are immediate execution orders on the market.

109. D. A limit order (buy limits sell limits) indicates that the order will be executed at a particular price or better if it hits that price.

110. D. A specific order is a buy-limit order.

111. C. A DMM cannot accept an NH.

112. A. It is an alternative order.

113. D. DMM maintains an organized and fair market on the NYSE trading floor.

114. A. Reverse splits cancel all stop and limit orders on the ex-split day. Open order is good-till-canceled (GTC).

115. A. It tracks the entire order of life from entry to execution.

116. A. Brokers use OATS to track the routing of OTC orders.

117. D. NYSE temporarily halts trading when the S&P declines 7% or more from the previous day's close.

118. A. Broker-dealers must keep corporate or partnership documents lifelong.

119. C. Dealers "back away" when they fail to honor a firm quote.

120. A. Entering an "at the open" order is not a violation.

121. B. FINRA rule 4513 states all complaints must be kept for four years.

122. D. U-forms of terminated employees are maintained for three years.

123. C. Records must be easily accessible for at least two years per FINRA and MSRB.

124. A. A control relationship must be disclosed at the time of recommendation to a potential security buyer per MSRB.

125. C. Cash dividends received on a margin account go entirely to the SMA.

Conclusion

Series 7 requires a thorough understanding and knowledge of US securities, banking, and financial trading. It is an interesting and exciting work arena where registered representatives help the public manage their wealth portfolios. A lot depends on their discretion, integrity, and efficiency. Qualifying for the Series 7 examination only helps you to step over the threshold.

If this guidebook helped you to achieve that significant mark, please leave a review on Amazon. Your appreciation and acknowledgment will help many others to benefit from this dedicated work.

References

Adam, H. (2019). *What is Maturity Date?* Investopedia. https://www.investopedia.com/terms/m/maturitydate.asp

Bloomenthal, A. (2023, June 10). *Inherited Stock: Definition, How It Works, and Example.* Investopedia. https://www.investopedia.com/terms/i/inherited-stock.asp

Boyte-White, C. (2023, December 20). *Are Catch-Up Contributions Included in the 415 Limit?* Investopedia. https://www.investopedia.com/ask/answers/112415/are-catchup-contributions-included-415-limit.asp

Chen, J. (2019). *What are Options? Types, Spreads, Example, and Risk Metrics.* Investopedia. https://www.investopedia.com/terms/o/option.asp

Chen, J. (2021, September 29). *At the Money (ATM): Definition & How It Works in Options Trading.* Investopedia. https://www.investopedia.com/terms/a/atthemoney.asp

Chen, J. (2022a, May 20). *Derivative Warrants Explained: Types and Example.* Investopedia. https://www.investopedia.com/terms/w/warrant.asp

Chen, J. (2022b, June 5). *Expiration Date (Derivatives) Definition.* Investopedia. https://www.investopedia.com/terms/e/expirationdate.asp

Chen, J. (2023, April 24). *How Options Work for Buyers and Sellers*. Investopedia. https://www.investopedia.com/terms/o/option.asp#:~:text=Options%20 are%20financial%20derivatives%20that

Dhir, R. (2021, March 21). *What It Means to Exercise a Contractual Right*. Investopedia. https://www.investopedia.com/terms/e/exercise.asp

Downey, L. (2022, July 14). *Underlying Security Definition*. Investopedia. https:// www.investopedia.com/terms/u/underlying-security.asp

Fernando, J. (2023, April 24). *Strike Price Definition*. Investopedia. https://www. investopedia.com/terms/s/strikeprice.asp

FINRA. (n.d.-a). *CONDUCT RULES (2000–3000) | FINRA.org*. Www.finra.org. Retrieved February 28, 2024, from https://www.finra.org/rules-guidance/ rulebooks/retired-rules-3

FINRA. (n.d.-b). *Taxation of Retirement Income | FINRA.org*. Www.finra.org. https://www.finra.org/investors/learn-to-invest/types-investments/ retirement/managing-retirement-income/taxation-retirement-income

FINRA. (2018, April 20). *Suitability | FINRA.org*. Finra.org. https://www.finra. org/rules-guidance/key-topics/suitability

FINRA. (2023, May 24). *Know What Triggers a Margin Call | FINRA.org*. Www. finra.org. https://www.finra.org/investors/insights/margin-calls

FINRA. (2024a). *2210. Communications with the Public | FINRA.org*. Www.fin-ra.org. https://www.finra.org/rules-guidance/rulebooks/finra-rules/2210

FINRA. (2024b). *FINRA Rulemaking Process | FINRA.org*. Www.finra.org. https://www.finra.org/rules-guidance/rulemaking-process

FINRA. (2024c, February 9). *Insurance | FINRA.org*. Www.finra.org. https:// www.finra.org/investors/investing/investment-products/insurance

Ganti, A. (2019). *How Implied Volatility (IV) Works With Options and Examples.* Investopedia. https://www.investopedia.com/terms/i/iv.asp

Investopedia Staff. (2023, August 13). *Everything You Need to Know About Junk Bonds.* Investopedia. https://www.investopedia.com/articles/02/052202.asp

Investor.gov. (n.d.). *Municipal Bonds | Investor.gov.* Www.investor.gov. https://www.investor.gov/introduction-investing/investing-basics/investment-products/bonds-or-fixed-income-products-0

Kagan, J. (2022, March 25). *Employee Retirement Income Security Act (ERISA).* Investopedia. https://www.investopedia.com/terms/e/erisa.asp

Kenton, W. (2019). *Option Premium: Definition, Factors Affecting Pricing, and Example.* Investopedia. https://www.investopedia.com/terms/o/option-premium.asp

Kenton, W. (2023, May 24). *Capital asset pricing model (CAPM) and assumptions explained.* Investopedia. https://www.investopedia.com/terms/c/capm.asp

Kurt, D. (2023, January 12). *How are capital gains and dividends taxed differently?* Investopedia. https://www.investopedia.com/ask/answers/12/how-are-capital-gains-dividends-taxed-differently.asp

Mitchell, C. (2022). *How In The Money (ITM) Options Work.* Investopedia. https://www.investopedia.com/terms/i/inthemoney.asp

Mitchell, C. (2023, January 10). *Out Of The Money (OTM) Definition and Example.* Investopedia. https://www.investopedia.com/terms/o/outofthemoney.asp

Schaub, A. (n.d.). *Lessons from FINRA's 2022 Report.* RegEd.com. Retrieved February 28, 2024, from https://www.reged.com/lessons-from-finras-2022-report/

SEC.gov | Self-Regulatory Organization Rulemaking. (n.d.). Www.sec.gov. Retrieved February 28, 2024, from https://www.sec.gov/rules/sro/msrb

Segal, T. (2021, March 21). *Why to Park Your Cash in a Money Market Fund.* Investopedia. https://www.investopedia.com/terms/m/money-marketfund.asp

Tamplin, T. (2023, May 30). *Call Risk | Definition, Causes, Types, How to Measure & Manage.* Finance Strategists. https://www.financestrategists.com/wealth-management/investment-risk/call-risk/

U.S. Securities and Exchange Commission. (n.d.-a). *Information is an investor's best tool.* https://www.sec.gov/investor/pubs/sec-guide-to-variable-annuities.pdf

U.S. Securities and Exchange Commission. (n.d.-b). *The Laws That Govern the Securities Industry | Investor.gov.* Www.investor.gov. https://www.investor.gov/introduction-investing/investing-basics/role-sec/laws-govern-securities-industry

U.S. Securities and Exchange Commission. (2010). *Mutual Funds and ETFS: A Guide for Investors Information is an investor's best tool.* https://www.sec.gov/investor/pubs/sec-guide-to-mutual-funds.pdf

Made in the USA
Coppell, TX
01 August 2024

35433202R00155